LA CUCINA ITALIANA

DELICIOUS

DESSERTS

LA CUCINA ITALIANA

DELICIOUS

DESSERTS

PRION

Published in the United Kingdom 1994 by
PRION,
an imprint of Multimedia Books Limited,
32-34 Gordon House Road, London NW5 1LP

Managing Editor: Anne Johnson
Design: Megra Mitchell
Production: Hugh Allan

A catalogue record for this book is available from
The British Library

ISBN 1 85375 148 0

10 9 8 7 6 5 4 3 2 1

Printed in Italy by New Interlitho

CONTENTS

PASTRIES

Italian pastries are a delight — both to the taste buds and to the eye.
They can be simple or elaborate, dainty or gargantuan, old favourites
or unusual new confections, suitable for a family meal or a special feast.
Rest assured, though, that whatever you choose,
it's guaranteed to be delicious.

Grape and Apple Cheesecake

Crostata di Mascarpone all'Uva e Mela

To serve 8

4 oz/100 g flour

2 oz/50 g caster sugar

a pinch of salt

4 oz/100 g butter

4 egg yolks

grated rind of 1 lemon

a little butter and flour for pie dish

7 oz/200 g Mascarpone cheese

2 oz/50 icing sugar

2 tablespoons brandy

20 small macaroons

a large bunch green grapes

1 apple

5 tablespoons caster sugar

5 mint leaves

Preparation and cooking time: about 1½ hours

To make the pastry, put the sifted flour, sugar and salt together in a bowl. Add the butter, cut into small cubes. Rub it in with your fingers until the mixture resembles coarse breadcrumbs. Add 2 egg yolks and the lemon rind. Roll the pastry into a ball, wrap it in cling film and leave it in the refrigerator for 30 minutes.

Meanwhile, preheat the oven to 375°F/190°C gas mark 5. Grease and flour a 10 inch/25 cm tart tin with a smooth bottom and fluted sides.

Roll out the pastry and line the tin, pricking the bottom with a fork. Bake in the oven for about 20 minutes or until well cooked and golden. Leave to cool in the tin.

Now prepare the filling. Beat the cheese and sifted icing sugar together, incorporating the 2 egg yolks, one at a time. Stir in the brandy.

Crumble the macaroons finely. When the pie shell is cold, take it out of the pie dish and set it on a plate. Sprinkle the macaroons over the bottom and pour in the filling. Wash and dry the grapes and arrange them on top together with thin slices of apple.

Dissolve the sugar in 1 tablespoon of water over low heat. When it is a thick syrup, brush it, still hot, over the fruit. Decorate the centre of the cake with the mint leaves and keep it in a cool place or the warmest part of the refrigerator until required. Serve within a couple of hours.

Plum Turnovers

Mezzelune alla Marmellata

To serve 6-8

12 oz/350 g flour, plus a little extra for the work surface and baking tray

¼ teaspoon baking powder

4 oz/100 g sugar

grated rind of ½ lemon

2 eggs

½ sachet of vanilla sugar

3 oz/75 g butter, plus a little extra for greasing the baking tray

2 tablespoons anise liqueur

1 jar plum jam

icing sugar

Preparation and cooking time: about 1½ hours

Sift the flour and baking powder together. Add the sugar and the grated lemon rind. Stir and then make a well in the centre. Place the eggs, vanilla sugar, butter (cut into little pieces) and the anise liqueur in the well. Combine with the flour to form a firm, smooth pastry. Preheat the oven to 350°F/180°C/gas mark 4.

Dust the work surface with a little flour and roll out the pastry to a thickness of ¼ inch/6 mm. Cut into 3 inch/7.5 cm circles with a serrated pastry cutter. Place 1 teaspoon of plum jam on each piece of pastry and fold each circle in half, sealing the edges.

Place the crescents on a buttered baking tray which has been sprinkled with a little flour. Make sure that they are not too close together as they will spread during baking.

Bake in the oven for 20 minutes. Leave to cool and sprinkle with a little icing sugar. Arrange on a dish and serve.

Strawberry and Apple Pie

Pie di Fragole e Mele

To serve 6

12 oz/350 g apples

1½ oz/40 g butter

2 oz/50 g caster sugar

3 tablespoons Maraschino liqueur

12 oz/350 g strawberries

2 soft Amaretti biscuits

6 soft sponge fingers

7 oz/200 g frozen puff pastry, defrosted

1 egg, beaten, for glazing

Preparation and cooking time: about 1 hour

Peel and core the apples, then cut them into small segments. In a large saucepan, melt the butter. Put in the apples, sprinkle with sugar and brown over high heat. Cook for about 2 minutes, then moisten with the Maraschino. Evaporate the liquid completely, and leave to cool.

Meanwhile, preheat the oven to 400°F/200°C/gas mark 6. Hull the strawberries, wash thoroughly and dry well. Cut into small segments and place in a round pie dish, together with the cold apples and the crumbled Amaretti biscuits and sponge fingers.

Roll out the pastry and use it to cover the pie dish, making sure it adheres well to the edges. Cut off the excess pastry and use the trimmings to make decorations on top of the pie. Arrange these on the pastry, glaze with the beaten egg and bake in the hot oven for about 30 minutes.

Place the pie dish on a serving plate and serve the pie straight from the dish.

Grape and Apple Cheesecake

Prune and Apple Tart

Crostata di Prugne e Mele

To serve 10

9 oz/250 g stoned prunes

4 fl oz/100 ml rum

7 oz/200 g butter, plus extra for greasing the tin

10 oz/300 g plain flour, plus extra for the work surface

1 egg

3 oz/75 g caster sugar, plus 3 tablespoons

$^1/_2$ teaspoon vanilla essence

a pinch of salt

1$^3/_4$ lb/800 g apples

1 oz/25 g butter

juice of $^1/_2$ lemon

flaked almonds

1 egg, beaten

icing sugar

Preparation and cooking time: about 2 hours

Soak the prunes in the rum for about 1 hour.

Work the butter and flour together, then place on a work surface and make a well in the centre. Break the egg into the centre and add the sugar, vanilla and salt. Mix quickly, using your fingertips so as not to over-soften the butter (which would make the pastry lose its body). Roll the pastry into a ball, wrap in cling film and refrigerate for 30 minutes.

Preheat the oven to 375°F/190°C/gas mark 5. To make the filling, peel and core the apples and dice finely. Place in a saucepan with the butter, lemon juice, 3 tablespoons caster sugar and a little cold water. Cover the pan and cook the apples over high heat for 7 minutes, then add the prunes and the rum they were soaked in. Cook until the prunes are quite dry and the apples are pulpy, then leave to cool.

On a lightly floured work surface, roll out the pastry into a circle $^1/_4$ inch/

6 mm thick. Use it to line a greased 10 inch/25 cm tart tin, cutting off the excess pastry. Pour the cooked fruit into the tart tin.

Re-roll the pastry trimmings, then, using a fluted cutter, cut into $^1/_2$ inch/ 1 cm wide strips. Arrange these in a lattice pattern on the fruit and fill the spaces with flaked almonds (about 20). Brush the pastry with beaten egg and sift over a light dusting of icing sugar. Bake in the hot oven for about 40 minutes. Serve the tart at room temperature.

Peach and Macaroon Pie

Crostata di Pesche all'Amaretto

To serve 6-8

a little butter and flour for pie dish

4 oz/100 g flour

a pinch of salt

2 oz/50 g sugar

grated rind of $^1/_2$ lemon

1 egg yolk

2 oz/50 g butter, softened

1 tablespoon dry vermouth

12 small macaroons

6 tablespoons peach jam

1 tablespoon apricot brandy

2 large yellow peaches

1 tablespoon Amaretto liqueur

a few sprigs of redcurrants

Preparation and cooking time: about 1 hour, plus cooling

Preheat the oven to 375°F/190°C/gas mark 5. Butter and flour a round 10 inch/25 cm pie dish.

Sift the flour and add the salt, sugar and the grated lemon rind. Make a well in the centre and add the egg yolk, the softened butter, cut into small pieces, and the vermouth. Knead rapidly into a smooth pastry, then roll out and line the prepared dish with it; prick the bottom of the pastry with a fork. Crumble over 7 macaroons. Set aside 2 tablespoons of jam, place the rest in a bowl and stir in the apricot brandy. Spread evenly over the crumbs.

Peel, halve and stone the peaches, then cut them into equal slices and arrange them in a circle, slightly overlapping on the pastry. In the centre put the remaining macaroons and sprinkle them with the Amaretto liqueur. Bake for about 40 minutes.

Remove the pie from the oven and let it cool in the dish, then place it on a large round plate. Melt the remaining jam over low heat, strain it through a fine sieve and brush the peach slices and the macaroons with it. As soon as the glaze has cooled and is firm, garnish the pie with sprigs of redcurrants and serve.

May Evening Pie

Crostata 'Sera di Maggio'

To serve 8

5 oz/150 g flour, plus extra for the dish

5 oz/150 g sugar

grated rind of ¹/₂ lemon

a pinch of salt

3 oz/75 g butter, softened, plus extra for the dish

1 small egg

¹/₂ oz/15 g leaf gelatine

1¹/₄ lb/600 g ripe strawberries

4 fl oz/100 ml Cointreau

¹/₄ pint/150 ml whipping cream

a few mint leaves for garnish

Preparation and cooking time: about 1 hour, plus 3-4 hours chilling

Mix the flour, 2 oz/50 g of the sugar, the grated lemon rind and salt together and make a well in the centre. Cut the softened butter into small pieces and place in the well with the egg; mix quickly to a smooth pastry. Roll it into a ball, wrap it in greaseproof paper or cling film and let it rest in the refrigerator for about 30 minutes.

Meanwhile, preheat the oven to 350°F/180°C/gas mark 4. Butter and flour a round pie dish 23 cm/9 inches in diameter. Roll out enough pastry to line the dish and prick it with a fork; cover it with a sheet of foil and place a few dried beans on top. Bake the pastry for about 30 minutes. Remove the beans and foil and let the pastry

shell cool inside the dish.

Dissolve the gelatine in a little cold water. Remove the stems from 1 lb/450 g of the strawberries, wash them in very cold water, drain them, then cut them into small pieces. Place them in a blender or food processor together with the remaining sugar and purée them, first at low speed then at high speed for a couple of minutes.

Heat the Cointreau in a saucepan; remove it from the heat and, while still hot, fold in the gelatine, stirring it until it is completely dissolved. Add the strawberries and stir the mixture for a further 30 seconds.

Turn out the pastry shell on to a serving dish and pour over the strawberry mixture, distributing it evenly. Keep the tart in the refrigerator for 3-4 hours or, even better, overnight, to set the filling.

A short time before serving, beat the whipping cream until stiff, then put it in a piping bag and decorate to taste, finishing off with the remaining strawberries, washed but not chopped, and a few mint leaves. Serve immediately.

Prune and Apple Tart (far left) and
Peach and Macaroon Pie (below)

Orange Tart with Whipped Cream

Crostata all'Arancia con Panna Montata

To serve 6-8

4 oz/100 g butter, softened, plus extra for tin

12 oz/350 g flour, plus extra for work surface and tin

1 egg, plus 4 yolks

4 oz/100 g icing sugar

1 teaspoon ground cinnamon

5 oz/150 g caster sugar

grated rind of 1 orange

18 fl oz/500 ml milk

2 tablespoons orange liqueur

4 oranges

¹/₃ pint/200 ml double cream, whipped

4 oz/100 g apricot jam

Preparation and cooking time: about 1¹/₂ hours

To prepare the pastry, beat the butter into 10 oz/300g of the flour, then place on a work surface and make a well in the centre. Break the egg into the centre and add the sugar and cinnamon. Knead fairly rapidly to avoid over-softening the butter, then wrap the pastry in cling film and leave to rest in the refrigerator for about 30 minutes.

Meanwhile, make the filling. In a bowl, work the egg yolks with the sugar, remaining 2 oz/50 g flour and grated orange rind. Heat the milk and pour it on to the egg mixture in a thin stream, then pour the custard back into the pan and place on the heat. Stirring continuously to avoid lumps, simmer for 5 minutes, then remove from the heat, stir in the liqueur and leave to cool.

Preheat the oven to 375°F/190°C/gas mark 5. On a lightly floured surface, roll out the pastry into a circle ⅛ inch/3 mm thick and use it to line a buttered and floured 10 inch/25 cm loose-bottomed tart tin. Fill with the orange-flavoured custard. Cut off the excess pastry and pinch up the edges of the crust. Bake the tart in the hot oven for about 40 minutes.

While the tart is baking, prepare the decoration. Peel 3 oranges, removing all the pith, and cut into rounds. Whip the cream until very stiff. Make a glaze by boiling the jam for 3 minutes with one-third of a glass of water. Peel the remaining orange and cut the rind into very thin strips. Blanch for 2 minutes, then drain very carefully.

Remove the tart from the oven, unmould it on to a serving plate and leave to cool. Arrange the orange rounds on the custard, and brush them with the tepid apricot glaze. Put the cream in a piping bag with a fluted nozzle, and pipe it around the edge of the tart, then arrange the strands of orange rind on top.

Frangipani Tartlets

Tartellette 'Frangipane'

To make 16

10 oz/300 g frozen shortcrust pastry

4 oz/100 g butter, softened and diced, plus extra for the tins

4 oz/100 g icing sugar

3 egg yolks

1 oz/25 g flour

4 oz/100 g blanched almonds, finely chopped

½ teaspoon vanilla essence

butter for greasing

Preparation and cooking time: about 1 hour

Defrost the shortcrust. Preheat the oven to 400°F/200°C/gas mark 6. Meanwhile, in a bowl, beat the diced softened butter with the icing sugar. Stir in the egg yolks, flour, chopped almonds and vanilla.

Grease 16 tartlet tins. Roll out the pastry to a thickness of ¼ inch/6 mm and use it to line the tins completely. Prick the pastry with a fork. Fill with the frangipani filling and bake in the hot oven for about 15 minutes.

As soon as the tartlets are baked, remove from the oven, invert and umould them. Arrange them carefully on a serving plate and serve warm.

Almond and Grape Flan

Sfogliata Amarettata all'Uva

To serve 10

10 oz/300 g puff pastry

butter for greasing

6 small macaroons

4 tablespoons red vermouth

about 1¼ lb/600 g white grapes

1 egg

3 oz/75 g caster sugar

¾ oz/20 g flour

1 sachet vanilla sugar

⅓ pint/200 ml milk

Preparation and cooking time: about 1¼ hours, plus any defrosting

Defrost the pastry if necessary. Roll it out and use it to line a buttered round 10 inch/25 cm quiche dish. Prick the bottom with a fork, then sprinkle over 5 finely crumbled macaroons. Moisten with the red vermouth and leave in a cool place. Preheat the oven to 375°F/190°C/gas mark 5.

Wipe the grapes with a damp cloth. Break the egg into a small saucepan, add 2 oz/50 g of sugar, the sieved flour and the vanilla sugar. Whisk to prevent lumps forming, then dilute the mixture with the cold milk, poured in a thin stream.

Bring the mixture to the boil, stirring all the time, then immediately pour it over the macaroons. Arrange the grapes on top, pushing them down slightly, in 4 concentric circles. Crumble the remaining macaroon and sprinkle it over the centre of the tart. Boil the remaining sugar with 1 tablespoon water to make a thick syrup, then bruish the grapes with it. Bake the tart in the preheated oven for about 40 minutes, then remove and allow it to cool in the dish before turning out and serving.

Orange Tart with Whipped Cream (opposite) and Frangipani Tartlets (above)

Pear Flan

Flan di Pere

To serve 6

4 oz/100 g flour

3 oz/75 g butter, softened

1¹/₂ oz/40 g caster sugar

1¹/₂ oz/40 g hazelnuts, finely chopped

¹/₂ teaspoon vanilla essence

a pinch of salt

3 large red pears

9 fl oz/250 ml dry red wine

10 oz/300 g caster sugar

1 cinnamon stick

a few black peppercorns

¹/₂ oz/12 g leaf gelatine, soaked in cold water

Preparation and cooking time: about 1 hour 20 minutes

Quickly knead the flour with the softened butter, sugar, chopped hazelnuts, vanilla and salt dissolved in 4 tablespoons water. Leave the pastry to rest in a cool place for 30 minutes.

Meanwhile, peel and halve the pears. Bring the wine to the boil with 9 fl oz/250 ml water, the sugar, cinnamon and peppercorns. Add the pears and cook for 6 minutes. Drain and leave to cool while you reduce the poaching syrup by half. Stir in the squeezed gelatine and make sure it has dissolved completely, then leave to cool.

Preheat the oven to 425°F/220°C/ gas mark 7. Roll out the pastry to a thickness of ¹/₈ inch/3 mm, prick with a fork, then use it to line the base and sides of a fluted 9 inch/23 cm flan tin. Cover with greaseproof paper, fill the tin with baking beans to prevent the pastry from puffing up during baking, and bake in the hot oven for about 20 minutes. Leave to cool, then fan out the pears on the cold pastry, pour over the wine glaze and serve.

Mascarpone Gougère (top) and Pear Flan (bottom)

Mascarpone Gougère

Gougère al Mascarpone

To serve 6

2 oz/50 g butter, plus a little for greasing

a pinch of salt

4 oz/100 g flour

3 eggs

5 oz/150 g mixed crystallized fruits, chopped

sugar crystals

3 oz/75 g caster sugar

2 egg yolks, beaten

5 oz/150 g Mascarpone cheese

port

5 oz/150 g plain chocolate, chopped or grated into flakes

Preparation and cooking time: about 1 hour 20 minutes

Preheat the oven to 400°F/200°C/gas mark 6. Bring to the boil 5 fl oz/150 ml water with 2 oz/50 g butter and the salt. Tip in the flour all at once and keep the pan on the heat, stirring continuously, until the mixture dries out slightly. Transfer to the bowl of an electric mixer fitted with a dough hook and leave to cool. Now mix in the eggs, one at a time, then the crystallized fruit.

On a greased baking sheet, place spoonfuls of the choux paste touching each other to form an 8 inch/20 cm crown. Sprinkle with sugar crystals and bake in the hot oven for 10 minutes, then reduce the heat to 350°F/180°C/gas mark 4 and bake for another 20 minutes.

To make the cream, cook the sugar with a drop of water to a temperature of 235°F/113°C. Gradually pour the syrup on to the egg yolks in a heatproof bowl, then add the Mascarpone and a small glass of port. Place the cream in the centre of the gougère crown and decorate with chopped or flaked chocolate.

Raspberry Tart

Crostata ai Lamponi

To serve 6

10 oz/300 g flour

5 oz/150 g butter, softened

5 oz/150 g caster sugar

a pinch of salt

2 eggs

1/2 teaspoon vanilla essence

1 oz/25 g flour

1 tablespoon cornflour

Cointreau

4 oz/100 g plain chocolate

4 oz/100 g raspberries

icing sugar

Preparation and cooking time: about 1 hour

To make the tart base, put the flour, softened butter, 2 oz/50 g of the sugar, salt and 3 fl oz/ 75 ml cold water in a bowl and quickly work together to make a pastry. Wrap in cling film and refrigerate for 30 minutes.

Meanwhile, make the filling. In an electric mixer, beat the eggs with the remaining sugar and vanilla until light and creamy, then sift in the flour and cornflour, a little at a time, and add a dash of Cointreau. Break the chocolate into a bowl and melt it in a tepid bain-marie.

Preheat the oven to 350°F/180°C/ gas mark 4. Roll out the pastry very thinly and use it to line a 10 inch/ 25 cm flan tin, crimping up the border. Line with greaseproof paper and fill with dried baking beans to prevent the pastry from puffing up during cooking. Bake in the preheated oven for 15 minutes, then take the tart base out of the oven and remove the paper and beans. Increase the oven temperature to 425°F/220°C/gas mark 7. Leaving the base in the tin, fill it with melted chocolate, half the raspberries and the filling. Decorate with the remaining raspberries, dust liberally with sifted icing sugar and return to the hot oven for about 10 minutes, checking that the sugar does not burn.

Unmould the tart on to a serving plate and serve cold, dusted with icing sugar.

Raspberry Tart

Ricotta Pie with Sultanas

Torta di Ricotta alla Panna

To serve 8

12 oz/350 g frozen shortcrust pastry, defrosted

a little flour for work surface and dish

a little butter for greasing

2 oz/50 g sultanas

4 oz/100 g candied peel

12 oz/350 g full-cream ricotta cheese

3 eggs, separated

4 oz/100 g sugar

grated rind of 1 lemon

a pinch of salt

a little icing sugar

Preparation and cooking time: about 1 hour, plus defrosting

Roll out the pastry on a lightly floured board and use it to line a buttered and floured 9 inch/23 cm tart tin. Cut off the excess pastry and shape into a ring, then use to thicken the sides of the pie. Prick the base with a fork.

Preheat the oven to 350°F/180°C/gas mark 4. Wash and dry the sultanas; cut the candied peel into small cubes. Sieve the ricotta into a bowl and mix in the egg yolks, one at a time, then the sugar, the lemon rind, the diced candied peel and the sultanas, stirring vigorously. Beat the egg whites with the salt until they are quite stiff and fold them into the mixture.

Pour the mixture into the pastry shell and tap the tin to remove air bubbles in the mixture. Bake for about 45 minutes. Finally, turn out and leave it to cool. Before serving, sprinkle with icing sugar.

Profiteroles in Spun Caramel

Piramide di Bignè

Makes about 40

4 oz/100 g butter, cut into pieces

a pinch of salt

7 oz/200 g flour, sifted

6 eggs, plus 2 egg yolks

a little butter for greasing

10 oz/300 g caster sugar

1 pint/600 ml milk

1 sachet of vanilla sugar

Preparation and cooking time: about 2 hours

Heat ¼ pint/150 ml of water, the butter and salt in a saucepan. As soon as it boils, remove from the heat and pour in 5 oz/150 g flour. Mix and then cook over low heat, stirring, until it no longer sticks to the edges of the pan. Turn out on to a working surface, spread out and leave to cool.

Preheat the oven to 375°F/190°C/gas mark 5. Return the mixture to the pan and mix in 4 eggs, one at a time. When the mixture is thick and smooth, spoon it into a piping bag. Pipe rosettes on to a buttered baking tray, making sure they are well separated. They will puff up and spread during baking.

Bake for 15 minutes. Before removing from the oven, cut open one profiterole to check that it is baked. It should be hollow and slightly crisp. Cool the profiteroles on a rack.

Meanwhile, beat together the remaining 2 eggs, egg yolks and half the sugar until the mixture forms soft white ribbons. Sift in the remaining

flour and add the cold milk and vanilla sugar. Heat gently and allow to thicken, stirring constantly. As soon as the mixture comes to the boil, plunge the pan into cold water to cool. Pipe the mixture into the profiteroles and arrange them on a serving plate.

Dissolve the remaining 5 oz/150g sugar in 4 tablespoons water over moderate heat. Let it boil until it has turned light brown, remove from the heat and stir to cool and thicken. When it begins to form threads, pour it over the profiteroles, holding the pan fairly high and moving it in circles so that the caramel falls in spun threads around the profiteroles. If it thickens too much, reheat it gently. Serve as soon as possible.

Lemon Cream Vol-au-vent

Vol-au-vent alla Crema di Limone

To make 8

8 large frozen vol-au-vent

butter for greasing

1 egg, beaten, for glazing

icing sugar

4 lemons

12 fl oz/350 ml milk

4 egg yolks

4 oz/100 g caster sugar

1 teaspoon cornflour

2 oz/50 g caster sugar

2 lemons

Preparation and cooking time: about 45 minutes

Preheat the oven to 425°F/220°C/gas mark 7. Arrange the still frozen vol-au-vent on a greased baking sheet. Brush with beaten egg and bake in the hot oven for 15-18 minutes. A couple of minutes before the end of baking, take them out of the oven for a moment, sprinkle with icing sugar and glaze under the grill. Remove the vol-au-vent as soon as they are lightly caramelized and leave to cool.

Meanwhile, prepare the lemon cream. Thoroughly wash 2 lemons and grate the rinds into the milk. Heat but do not boil. In a bowl, mix together the egg yolks, caster sugar and cornflour, then gradually strain on the hot milk, return to the pan and set over very low heat. Heat the lemon cream until thickened, stirring continuously, but do not let it boil. Take the pan off the heat and leave to cool.

Meanwhile, wash the remaining 2 lemons, pare off the rinds and cut into slivers. Blanch in boiling water for 2 minutes and drain.

Make a caramel with the 2 oz/50 g sugar and 2 fl oz/50 ml water. Fill the vol-au-vent with the tepid lemon cream, garnish with lemon slivers and drizzle on the caramel. Arrange on a plate and serve.

Profiteroles in Spun Caramel (opposite) and ***Lemon Cream Vol-au-vent*** *(above)*

Amaretto Tart

Crostata all'Amaretto

To serve 8

10 oz/300 g flour

4 oz/100 g butter, softened and diced

1 egg, plus 6 extra yolks

4 oz/100 g icing sugar

¹/₂ teaspoon vanilla essence

12 soft Amaretti biscuits

10 oz/300 g Mascarpone cheese

flour and butter for the work surface and tin

13 small Amaretti biscuits

rum

¹/₃ pint/200 ml whipping cream

cocoa powder

Preparation and cooking time: about 1 hour 40 minutes

First make the pastry. Mix the flour with the butter and make a well in the centre. Add the egg and one yolk, then add the sugar and vanilla. Knead quickly so that the butter does not become too warm, then form the pastry into a ball, wrap in cling film and refrigerate for about 30 minutes.

Now prepare the filling. Crush the 12 soft Amaretti biscuits in a food processor, pulsing the motor for only 1 or 2 seconds so as not to crush them too finely. In a bowl, combine the Mascarpone, 5 egg yolks and crushed biscuits. Mix together until smooth and blended.

Preheat the oven to 400°F/200°C/gas mark 6. Take the pastry out of the fridge, remove the cling film and lightly flour the work surface. Roll out the pastry into a circle ¹/₈ inch/3 mm thick. Grease and flour a10 inch/ 25 cm tart tin and line it with the pastry. Fill with the cheese mixture and bake in the preheated oven for about 50 minutes. Remove the tart from the oven, unmould it on to a pastry rack and leave to cool.

Just before serving, decorate the tart with small Amaretti biscuits sprinkled with rum. Whip the cream and, using a piping bag with a fluted nozzle, pipe on rosettes of cream. Sift over a dusting of cocoa and serve.

Raisin and Pine Nut Tart

Crostata di Uvetta e Pinoli

To serve 8

12 oz/350 g frozen shortcrust pastry

4 oz/100 g raisins

¹/₂ glass rum

flour and butter for the work surface and tin

2 oz/50 g pine nuts

6 egg yolks

5 oz/150 g caster sugar

¹/₃ pint/200 ml whipping cream

¹/₂ teaspoon vanilla essence

icing sugar for dusting

Preparation and cooking time: about 50 minutes, plus defrosting the pastry

Defrost the pastry and soak the raisins in the rum.

When the pastry has defrosted, preheat the oven to 375°F/190°C/gas mark 5. On a floured surface, roll out the pastry. Grease and flour a10¹/₂ inch/26 cm tart tin and line it with the pastry, pinching it up along the border.

Drain the raisins from the rum, squeeze dry and lay over the pastry case. Place the pine nuts on top.

In a bowl, beat the egg yolks with the sugar, cream and vanilla. Pour this mixture over the raisins and pine nuts and bake the tart in the preheated oven for about 45 minutes. Unmould and serve warm or cold, with a dusting of icing sugar.

Pear Cake

Torta di Pere

To serve 8

7 oz/200 g butter, softened

5 oz/150 g icing sugar, plus a little extra for dusting

3 eggs

4 oz/100 g flour

2 oz/50 g cornflour

¹/₂ teaspoon vanilla essence

rum essence

grated rind of 1 lemon

1 lb 2 oz/500 g pears

butter and flour for the tin

Preparation and cooking time: about 1¹/₄ hours

Preheat the oven to 375°F/190°C/gas mark 5. With an electric mixer, beat the softened butter with the icing sugar until soft and fluffy. Add the eggs and, when they are completely amalgamated, sift in the flour and cornflour. Flavour with the vanilla, 3-4 drops of rum essence and the grated rind of a well-washed lemon.

For a perfect tart, choose absolutely ripe pears. If they are under-ripe, they will not cook properly, and if over-ripe, they will give off too much juice during baking.

Peel the pears and slice thinly. Grease and flour a 10 inch/25 cm springform tin. Add about half the

pears to the egg mixture, pour into the tin and arrange the remaining pears on the surface. Bake in the preheated oven for about 1 hour 10 minutes.

Unmould the tart on to a serving dish and leave to cool slightly. Sift on a thin layer of icing sugar and serve.The tart should be eaten almost as soon as it comes out of the oven.

Amaretto Tart (opposite), **Raisin and Pine Nut Tart** (top) and **Pear Cake** (above)

Fruit Vol-au-Vent

Sfogliata alla Frutta

To serve 8

1 lb 2 oz/500 g frozen puff pastry

9 fl oz/250 ml mik

grated rind of 1 lemon

2 egg yolks

3 oz/75 g sugar

¹/₂ teaspoon vanilla essence

1 oz/25 g flour

flour and butter for the work surface and baking sheet

1 egg, beaten, for glazing

1 lb/450 g plums

14 oz/400 g apricots

10 oz/300 g peaches

3 oz/75 g strawberries

1 slice of watermelon, about 1lb 2 oz/ 500 g

4 fl oz/100 ml whipping cream

Preparation and cooking time: about 2 hours

Make the custard while you defrost the pastry. Heat the milk with the lemon rind. In a bowl, mix the egg yolks with the sugar, vanilla and flour. Gradually stir in the hot, but not boiling, milk, then return the custard to the saucepan you used for the milk and, stirring continuously to avoid lumps, simmer the custard over very moderate heat for 3 - 4 minutes. Take the pan off the heat and leave to cool.

Preheat the oven to 400°F/200°C/ gas mark 6. On a lightly floured surface, roll out the pastry to a thickness of about ¹/₄ inch/6 mm and cut out two 10 inch/25 cm circles. Cut out a 1¹/₄ inch/3 cm border from one circle. Brush the larger circle with beaten egg and lay the border on top to make a vol-au-vent. Brush again with egg, then transfer to a greased baking sheet and bake in the preheated oven for about 25 minutes.

Meanwhile, stone all the fruit. Reserve 7 oz/200 g plums and 4 oz/100 g apricots, and cut the rest into small pieces. Scoop out the watermelon seeds.

Whip the cream until very stiff and mix it into the cold custard. To assemble the tart, place the cold pastry case on a serving plate, then fill it with pieces of fruit, almost all the watermelon and the custard. Decorate the tart with the remaining fruit. Keep in the fridge until ready to serve

Cherry Puff

Sfogliata di Vignola

To serve 6

14 oz/400 g frozen puff pastry

¹/₂ pint/300 ml milk

¹/₂ teaspoon vanilla essence

grated rind of 1 lemon

3 egg yolks

3¹/₂ oz/90 g caster sugar

1 oz/25 g flour

10 oz/300 g cherries

butter for greasing

1 tablespoon icing sugar

Preparation and cooking time: about 55 minutes, plus defrosting the pastry

Defrost the pastry. Meanwhile, prepare the pastry cream. Heat the milk with the vanilla and lemon rind. In a bowl, beat the egg yolks with the

sugar and flour. Gradually pour in the hot, but not boiling, milk, stirring to prevent lumps from forming. Return the custard to the milk pan and set over very moderate heat. Simmer for 3 - 4 minutes, stirring continuously, then take off the heat and leave to cool.

Preheat the oven to 400°F/200°C/gas mark 6. Rinse the cherries under running water, drain well and stone with a cherry stoner. Roll out the pastry into 2 equal rectangles. Spread the cold pastry cream over one and scatter on the cherries. Cover with the other pastry rectangle and seal the edges so that the filling does not seep out.

Place the cherry puff on a greased baking sheet and bake in the preheated oven for about 45 minutes. Remove from the oven as soon as it is baked and transfer to a serving plate. Serve slightly warm, sprinkled with icing sugar.

Chocolate Tartlets

Tartelette Farcite

To make 20

4 oz/100 g butter

7 oz/200 g flour, plus extra for work surface

6 oz/175 g icing sugar

almond essence

9 oz/250 g Mascarpone cheese

2 tablespoons Kirsch

grated rind of 1 orange

5 oz/150 g plain chocolate

Preparation and cooking time: about 1 hour

First prepare the tartlet cases (this can be done the day before). Mix the butter with the flour and 4 oz/100 g of the sugar, then place on the work surface and make a well in the centre. Pour 1½ fl oz/40 ml cold water and a few drops of almond essence into the centre and knead quickly, using only your fingertips, so as not to warm the butter too much. Wrap the pastry in cling film and refrigerate for about 30 minutes. Preheat the oven to 400°F/200°C/gas mark 6.

Roll out the pastry on a lightly floured work surface into a ⅛ inch/3 mm thick circle and use it to line twenty 2½ inch/6 cm tartlet tins. Arrange these on a baking sheet and bake in the hot oven for about 10 minutes. Remove the tartlets from the oven, unmould them and leave to cool.

Meanwhile, prepare the filling. Put the Mascarpone in a bowl and sift in the remaining icing sugar from a height. Mix together and flavour with the Kirsch, orange rind and 1½ oz/40 g of the chocolate, grated. Put the filling in a piping bag fitted with a plain nozzle and pipe it into the tartlet cases.

Melt the remaining chocolate in a bain-marie and leave to cool almost completely, without hardening again. Place in a piping cone and decorate the tartlets. As each one is ready, place it on a serving plate and serve immediately.

Fruit Vol-au-vent (opposite) , Cherry Puff (top) and Chocolate Tartlets (right)

FRUIT

Fruit must have been Man's earliest dessert. It is certainly one of the most versatile ingredients we have on offer and can be used in a multitude of ways. Modern transportation makes fresh fruit easily obtainable all year round, regardless of the season. With all the options available, the only problem is what to do with it. The choice is yours ...

DESSERTS

Netted Plums

Prugne Nella Rete

To serve 4

butter and flour for the work surface and tin

1 oz/30 g butter

3 eggs, plus 1 egg yolk

14 oz/400 g sugar

grated rind of 1 lemon

a little vanilla sugar

2 oz/50 g cornflour

4 oz/100 g flour

10 large yellow plums

4 fl oz/ 100 ml dry white wine

7 oz/200 g plum jam

¹/₃ pint/200 ml Amaretto liqueur

Preparation and cooking time: about 2 hours

Preheat the oven to 350°F/180°C/gas mark 4. To make a sponge, grease and flour a 9 inch/23 cm dome-shaped cake tin. Melt the butter and leave it to cool while beating together the 3 whole eggs and the yolk with 8 oz/225 g of the sugar, until the mixture is light and fluffy. Stir in the grated lemon rind, vanilla sugar, cornflour and most of the sifted flour. Lastly, add the cool melted butter.

Pour the mixture into the prepared cake tin and bake it in the oven for 35 minutes, or until a skewer inserted into the centre comes out clean. Cool on a wire rack.

While the sponge is baking, wash and dry the plums, then cut them in half, remove the stones and place them in a pan in a single layer. Sprinkle with 1 oz/25 g of sugar, add the white wine and cook them over moderate heat with the lid on for 5 minutes. Take them out of the pan and drain them on kitchen towels. Add the plum jam and half the liqueur to the juice left in the pan. Stir over low heat until it becomes a thick syrup.

When the sponge is cool, cut it into three layers, moisten them with the remaining liqueur, then spread with the jam mixture (reserving 2 tablespoons) and re-assemble the gâteau on a serving plate. Spread the remaining jam on top and cover it with the cooked plum halves. Leave it in a cool place (not the refrigerator) while you prepare the caramel.

To make the caramel, place the remaining sugar with 3 tablespoons of water over low heat, stirring gently at first until the sugar is completely dissolved. Cook until the sugar completely caramelizes. Dip a wooden spoon into the caramel and run it crisscross fashion over all the plums, like an irregular net. Serve immediately.

Oranges in Grand Marnier

Arance al Grand Marnier

To serve 4

6 large ripe oranges, washed

6 sugar cubes

4 tablespoons Grand Marnier

Preparation and cooking time: about 30 minutes, plus 30 minutes' chilling

Pierce the washed oranges all over with a needle. Rub every side of a sugar cube over each orange. Place the sugar in a saucepan. Peel the oranges, remove all the pith and divide them into segments in a bowl. Squeeze any juice remaining in the peel over the sugar cubes.

Heat the sugar cubes gently until dissolved. When a light syrup has formed, remove the pan from the heat and pour in the Grand Marnier. Stir and allow to cool. Pour the liquid over the orange segments and refrigerate for 30 minutes before serving.

If you like, you can place the oranges in individual goblets and garnish to taste.

Bananas with Pistachios

Banane 'Rosate' al Pistacchio

To serve 4

4 ripe bananas

1 oz/25 g sugar

4 tablespoons rum

1 oz/25 g pistachio nuts

a pinch of salt

5 tablespoons red fruit or rose hip jam

4-5 rose petals

Preparation time: about 20 minutes

Peel the bananas and halve them lengthways. Arrange them on a large dish and sprinkle with the sugar and rum. Leave to stand in a cool place.

Meanwhile, par-boil the pistachios in salted water for a couple of minutes. Peel them while they are still hot and chop them finely. Put the jam into a bowl and stir until smooth. Place it in the centre of a serving dish and arrange the bananas around it. Pour the rum marinade over the bananas and top with the pistachios.

Garnish with 4-5 fresh rose petals (if available) and serve immediately.

Netted Plums

Strawberry Mould

Sformato di Fragole

To serve 6

13 oz/375 g strawberries

7¹/₂ oz/215 g caster sugar

juice of ¹/₂ lemon

9 fl oz/250 ml milk

lemon rind

2 egg yolks

1 oz/25 g flour

¹/₂ teaspoon vanilla essence

¹/₄ pint /150ml double cream

soft sponge fingers

4 oz/100 g egg whites (about 4 egg whites)

a pinch of salt

Preparation and cooking time: about 1 hour, plus chilling

Hull and wash 10 oz/300 g of the strawberries, reserving the rest for decoration. Place in a bowl and sprinkle 2 oz/50 g of the sugar and the lemon juice. Cover and leave to marinate in a cool place.

To make the pastry cream, heat the milk with a strip of well-washed lemon rind. In a bowl, mix the egg yolks with 3 oz/75 g sugar, the flour and vanilla. Pour in the hot, but not boiling, milk in a steady stream, pour the mixture back into the milk pan and set over low heat. Simmer, stirring continuously, for 3-4 minutes. Take off the heat and leave to cool, stirring from time to time to prevent a skin forming.

To assemble the dessert, whip the cream very stiffly and fold it into the pastry cream. Remove the strawberries from the marinade and brush the sponge fingers with the liquid.

In a bowl, make alternating layers of sponge fingers, marinated strawberries and pastry cream, ending with a layer of sponge fingers. Cover with cling film and chill in the refrigerator for at least 6 hours.

Shortly before serving, make the meringue. Preheat the oven to 475°F/240°C/gas mark 9. Beat the egg whites with the salt until very firm, then delicately fold in the remaining sugar. Place this mixture in a piping bag fitted with a fluted nozzle. Invert the dessert on to an ovenproof serving dish and pipe the meringue all over it. Place it in the oven until just lightly browned, decorate with the remaining strawberries and serve immediately.

Melon Bavarian Cream

Bavarese di Melone

To serve 8-10

³/₄ oz/20 g powdered gelatine

1 perfectly ripe medium melon

3 oz/75 g sugar

2 oz/50 g cleaned redcurrants

1 sachet of vanilla sugar

¹/₃ pint/200 ml whipping cream

2 oz/50 g strawberry jam

Preparation and cooking time: about 1¹/₄ hours, plus at least 2 hours' chilling

Dissolve the gelatine in cold water. Wash and dry the melon, then halve it and remove the seeds. Remove the pulp with a spoon, without piercing the rind which will be used as a container.

Place the pulp in a saucepan and add the sugar and the redcurrants. Place the saucepan on the heat and,

stirring occasionally with a wooden spoon, simmer gently until the mixture has the consistency of jam, making sure it does not stick to the bottom of the pan.

Remove from the heat, stir the mixture for a couple of minutes and pour it into a bowl. While it is still warm, stir in the vanilla sugar and the gelatine. Mix well to dissolve the gelatine, then let the mixture cool. Whip the cream and fold it into the melon cream when it is cold but not yet firm, mixing with a motion from top to bottom rather than round and round (to prevent the cream from going flat). Pour the strawberry jam into a small bowl and stir vigorously with a spoon to make it smooth.

Spread a layer of the melon Bavarian cream in each half shell of the melon and pour over each layer some of the strawberry jam. Refrigerate for at least 2 hours so that the Bavarian cream will firm, then cut each half into 4-5 slices, using a very sharp knife; arrange them on a serving plate and serve.

Fruit and Nut Surprise

Pesche ai Pinoli

To serve 4

4 ripe, equal-sized yellow peaches

a knob of butter

1 clove

2 inch/5 cm piece lemon rind

2 tablespoons sugar

6 tablespoons brandy

8 tablespoons pine nuts

Preparation and cooking time:
about 45 minutes

Remove the stems from the peaches, then wash and dry them. Cut them in half with a small sharp knife and remove the stones.

Melt a large knob of butter in a saucepan, then arrange the 8 peach halves on the bottom of the pan, cut sides down. Fry very gently for a few moments with the pan uncovered, then add the clove and the piece of lemon rind. Sprinkle the fruit with the sugar and moisten with the brandy. Move the pan slightly to make sure the peaches do not stick to the bottom, then lower the heat to the minimum, cover, and cook the peaches for about 20 minutes until they are poached and glazed.

Place the peaches, cut sides upwards, on a serving dish and, in the hollow of each, place a spoonful of pine nuts. Reduce the cooking liquid slightly, then strain it directly on to the fruit.

Serve immediately while still hot – though peaches prepared in this way are also excellent lukewarm.

Strawberry Mould (far left); **Melon Bavarian Cream** (above)

Baskets of Grapes

Cestini all'Uva

To make 6

2 egg whites

3 oz/75 g sugar

1 oz/25 g flour

2 oz/50 g butter, melted

butter and flour for baking tray

1 lb/450 g vanilla ice cream

9 fl oz/275 ml whipping cream

a large bunch of black grapes

Preparation and cooking time:
45 minutes

Preheat the oven to 425°F/220°C/gas mark 7. Beat the egg whites in a bowl until stiff, then gradually whisk in the sugar and keep beating for 2-3 minutes. Add the flour and the melted butter, stirring to form a smooth batter.

Grease and flour a baking tray. Pour about 3 tablespoons of the batter separately on to it, keeping them well apart. Spread the mixture on the tray with the back of a spoon into 3 thin omelettes about 5 inches/12 cm in diameter. Bake for 6-7 minutes until golden at the edges.

Remove them from the oven and, working quickly with a fish slice, transfer each on to an up-turned glass.While soft, press them against the glass bottom to shape into baskets. Repeat with the remaining mixture. Set aside, still on the glasses, to firm up.

When cool and firm put a scoop of ice cream in the centre of each basket. Decorate with whipped cream and garnish all around with the washed and dried grapes. Serve at once.

Redcurrants in Lemon Baskets

'Cestini' con Crema e Ribes

To serve 4

5 large lemons, washed

2 small macaroons

3 egg yolks

4 oz/100 g sugar

1 oz/25 g flour

1/2 pint/300 ml milk

1 tablespoon orange liqueur

8 bunches redcurrants

8 fresh mint leaves

7 rolled wafers

Preparation and cooking time: about 1 hour

Grate the rind of one lemon. Halve the other 4 lemons and squeeze them, reserving the juice. Scrape out the flesh and trim the bases so that they stand level.

Crumble the macaroons and divide them among the lemon halves. Add egg yolks, sugar, flour and 2 tablespoons of the milk to the pan with the lemon rind, and beat to obtain a perfectly smooth mixture. Add the rest of the milk and, stirring continuously, bring to the boil. Remove from the heat and add the liqueur, then stand the pan in cold water and stir until the custard is completely cooled.

Wash the redcurrants and dry them on a cloth. Pick off the largest currants and arrange them over the macaroon crumbs in the lemon halves; fill up with the lemon cream, using a piping bag with a plain round nozzle. Garnish with redcurrants and a mint leaf and arrange on a flat dish, interspersed with the wafers. Serve immediately, before the cream can absorb any bitterness from the lemon pith.

If you do not wish to use lemon halves as containers, you could substitute individual pastry shells baked blind with dried beans to keep their shape. The baskets will also need to be served quickly, before the pastry loses its crispness.

Apple Abundance

Mele Golose

To serve 10

10 apples, equal in size and not too ripe

1 oz/25 g blanched almonds

1 oz/25 g blanched hazelnuts

1 oz/25 g shelled and skinned peanuts

1 oz/25 g blanched walnuts

1 oz/25 g plain chocolate, broken into pieces

butter for the dish

1 small cinnamon stick

3 cloves

spiral of lemon rind, 3 inch/7.5 cm long

1/4 pint/150 ml sweet white wine

5 oz/150 g caster sugar

4 egg yolks

1 oz/25 g cornflour

a little vanilla sugar

a pinch of salt

1 pint/600 ml milk

4 tablespoons Calvados or brandy

1 oz/25 g pistachio nuts

1/4 pint/150 ml whipping cream

Preparation and cooking time: about 1 1/2 hours, plus chilling

Peel the apples and, using an apple corer, cut into the bases, stopping when you reach the stalks: you should hollow out the cores just up to the stalk ends, leaving each closed at the top. Remove the apple flesh from the cores, chop it and add to the puréed nuts and chocolate in the bowl, and mix together well.

Stuff each apple with the mixture, pressing it in with a teaspoon. Butter an ovenproof dish which is just the right size to hold the apples in one layer and arrange them in it. Break up the cinnamon stick and put this in the dish, along with the cloves and the lemon rind. Pour in the wine and sprinkle over 2 oz/50 g of the sugar. Bake in the oven for about 45 minutes, basting from time to time with the juices.

Remove the cooked apples from the oven and set them aside while you prepare the custard. Beat the egg yolks in a saucepan with the remaining sugar, cornflour, vanilla sugar and salt. Then pour in the milk in a slow trickle, mixing constantly with a small whisk. Bring to the boil, remove from the heat and add the Calvados or brandy. Arrange the apples on a serving dish and pour the custard over them at once.

Blanch the pistachio nuts in boiling salted water, then chop them and sprinkle them over the custard-covered apples. Whip the cream until it is stiff and put it in a piping bag. Decorate the apples with swirls around the outside and one in the centre. Keep in a very cool place or in the least cold part of the refrigerator until you are ready to serve.

Semolina and Pear Moulds

Sformatini Semolino e Pere

To serve 6

1³/₄ pints/1 litre milk

7 oz/200 g caster sugar, plus a few extra spoonfuls for the moulds

¹/₂ teaspoon vanilla essence

grated rind of ¹/₂ lemon

7 oz/200 g semolina

1¹/₄ lb/600 g pears

2 oz/50 g butter

1 tablespoon rum

4 egg yolks

4 oz/100 g fresh or frozen raspberries

4 fl oz/100 ml whipping cream

Preparation and cooking time: about 45 minutes

Bring the milk to the boil, then add 3 oz/75 g of the sugar, the vanilla and lemon rind. Scatter in the semolina from above, mixing well to avoid lumps forming. Cook for 10 minutes, stirring continuously.

Peel and core the pears and dice the flesh finely. Heat 1 oz/25 g of the butter with 1 tablespoon of the remaining sugar in a frying pan. Add the diced pears and sauté for about 3 minutes, taking care that they do not disintegrate. Flavour with the rum, then take off the heat.

Grease 6 crème caramel moulds or ramekins and coat with a sprinkling of sugar. Add the egg yolks to the semolina mixture, one by one, stirring until completely amalgamated. Pour 2 tablespoons of semolina into each mould, then make a layer of half the pears. Repeat the layering, ending with a layer of semolina.

Stand the moulds in a bain-marie of hot, but not boiling, water, and cook in the oven at 375°F/190°C/gas mark 5 for 30 minutes.

Meanwhile, prepare the sauce. Purée the raspberries in a blender with the remaining sugar and the cream. Pour into a small saucepan and heat the sauce until thickened.

Carefully unmould the semolina moulds, taking care not to break them, and pour over the hot sauce. Serve at once.

Baked Peaches

Pesche al Forno

To serve 8

4 large peaches, about 1³/₄lb/800 g

3 tablespoons caster sugar

1 glass full-bodied red wine

1 oz/25 g blanched almonds

2 oz/50 g shelled hazelnuts

8 Amaretti biscuits

¹/₃ pint/200 ml whipping cream

vanilla ice cream

Preparation and cooking time: about 1 hour

Preheat the oven to 400°F/200°C/gas mark 6. Halve the peaches along the lines running down their sides and remove the stones. Arrange the unpeeled peach halves, rounded sides up, in an ovenproof dish. Sprinkle with the sugar and moisten with the wine. Bake in the preheated oven for about 20 minutes.

Meanwhile, finely crush the almonds, hazelnuts and Amaretti biscuits in a food processor and tip them on to a sheet of greaseproof paper. Take the peaches out of the oven, drain off the cooking liquid, then arrange the peaches on a serving plate and leave to cool.

Whip the cream until very stiff. Place the ice cream in an immaculately clean wooden bowl and leave to soften. With an ice cream scoop, make 8 balls and roll them in the crushed nut mixture, then place a ball in the cavity of each peach half.

Put the whipped cream into a piping bag with a fluted nozzle, and pipe a ribbon of cream around the balls of ice cream. Serve immediately.

Semolina and Pear Moulds (left) **and** *Baked Peaches* (below)

Tropical Fig Delight

Fichi Speziati con Ribes e Gelato

To serve 6

2¼ lb/1 kg fresh figs, not over-ripe

4 oz/100 g sugar

2 oz/50 g sultanas

a large pinch of ground cinnamon

a large pinch of ground ginger

a few whole cloves

6 tablespoons brandy

rind of 1 lemon

12 thin slices fruit cake or loaf

redcurrants

6 scoops vanilla ice cream

Preparation and cooking time: about 40 minutes, plus 1 hour marinating

Using a small, sharp knife, peel the figs. Cut each one into 4 or 6 pieces according to size and place in a stainless steel saucepan. Add the sugar, sultanas, cinnamon, ginger and a few cloves. Pour over 2 tablespoons of the brandy. Cut a 3 inch/7.5 cm piece of lemon rind into needle-fine strips and add to the saucepan. Cover the mixture and leave in a cool place for about 1 hour.

Cook the figs over low heat for about 15 minutes from the moment the liquid begins to simmer. Keep the pan uncovered and stir gently from time to time. Immerse the saucepan in cold water to cool quickly.

Arrange the fruit cake in a glass salad bowl and pour over the remaining brandy. Spread the fig mixture on top and cover. Keep in the refrigerator until it is time to serve. Then sprinkle some stemmed washed redcurrants on top and add scoops of ice cream.

Strawberry Flan

Torta Ripiena alle Fragole

To serve 12

4 eggs, plus 2 extra yolks

10 oz/300 g caster sugar

a pinch of salt

1¹/₂ teaspoons vanilla essence

5 oz/150 g flour

butter and flour for the tin

¹/₃ pint/200 ml milk

grated rind of 1 lemon

9 oz/250 g strawberries, plus 6 for decoration

3 fl oz/75 ml Maraschino liqueur

¹/₂ pint/300 ml whipping cream

icing sugar

Preparation and cooking time: about 2 hours

First make a sponge cake for the base. (This can be done 3 or 4 days in advance.) Preheat the oven to 350°F/180°C/gas mark 4. Whisk the 4 eggs with half the sugar, the salt and ¹/₂ teaspoon vanilla, using a hand-held or electric mixer, until of a ribbon consistency. Sift in the flour from a height; then fold it in delicately from bottom to top and vice-versa, using a scrupulously clean spoon.

Grease a 10 inch/25 cm springform tin and dust with a little flour. Spoon in the sponge mixture and bake in the preheated oven for about 25 minutes. As soon as the cake is ready, unmould it on to a pastry rack and leave to cool.

Meanwhile, make the custard. Heat the milk with the lemon rind and remaining vanilla. In a bowl, beat the egg yolks with 2 oz/50g sugar. Gradually stir in the hot, but not boiling, milk, then return the custard to the saucepan you used for the milk

and set over very moderate heat. Stirring continuously, heat the custard until thickened, without letting it boil, or it will curdle. As soon as it is ready, take off the heat and leave to cool.

To prepare the strawberry sauce, purée 4 oz/100 g of the strawberries with the remaining sugar at maximum speed and place in a bowl. Now make the filling. Hull the remaining strawberries and cut into small pieces. Place in a bowl and macerate with 1 fl oz/25 ml Maraschino. Meanwhile, whip the cream until very stiff, adding a spoonful of icing sugar.

To assemble the flan, hollow out the centre of the sponge cake, reserving the crumbs. Moisten the cake with the remaining Maraschino diluted with 1¹/₂ fl oz/40 ml water, then fill it with the macerated strawberries, about one-third of the whipped cream and the cake crumbs. Level the surface to restore the cake to its original shape.

Put the remaining cream into a piping bag with a fluted nozzle and pipe out 2 stripes to divide the cake into 2 'semi-circles'. Fill the space between the stripes with the custard and decorate with halved strawberries. Cover the 'semi-circles' with the sauce, and pipe rosettes of cream all around the edge. Place the flan on a serving plate and serve.

Strawberry Pillow

Mattonella Fragolina

To serve 6

3 eggs, size 2 or 3

4 oz/100 g caster sugar

a pinch of salt

1/2 teaspoon vanilla essence

4 oz/100 g flour

butter and flour for the tin

1 1/2 fl oz/40 ml Maraschino liqueur

9 fl oz/250 ml whipping cream

1 tablespoon icing sugar

10 oz/300 g strawberries

3 oz/75 g caster sugar

Preparation and cooking time: about 1 1/4 hours

First make a sponge. (You can make it 4 or 5 days in advance and keep it wrapped in cling film.) Preheat the oven to 350°F/180°C/gas mark 4. Whisk the eggs with the sugar and salt, using a hand-held or electric mixer, to a ribbon consistency. Stir in the vanilla, then fold in the flour delicately, working from bottom to top and vice-versa. Grease and flour a rectangular 12 x 5 inch/30 x 12 cm cake tin and pour in the sponge mixture. Bake in the preheated oven for about 35 minutes. Check that the sponge is cooked by inserting a wooden skewer into the centre. When it comes out dry, take the sponge out of the oven and leave in the tin for 5 minutes, then unmould it on to a pastry rack and leave to cool.

To assemble the pillow, split the sponge cake lengthways and moisten the two halves with the Maraschino diluted with 1 1/2 fl oz/40 ml cold water. Whip the cream until stiff and sweeten with the icing sugar.

Spoon about half the cream on to

one sponge rectangle. Hull, wash, drain and slice the strawberries, and arrange 7 oz/200 g of them on top of the cream. Cover with the other sponge rectangle. Purée the remaining strawberries with the caster sugar to make a thick sauce. Fill a piping bag with a fluted nozzle with the remaining whipped cream, and pipe a border of cream swirls all round the edge of the dessert. Pour the sauce over the middle of the dessert to fill this border, transfer to a serving plate and serve immediately.

Strawberry Mousse

Turbante Rosa Fragola

To serve 8-10

2 tablespoons powdered gelatine

a little almond oil

8 oz/250 g just-ripe strawberries

4 oz /100 g sugar

3/4 pint/500 ml whipping cream

4 tablespoons Cointreau

2 tablespoons desiccated coconut

10 equal-sized strawberries, with their stalks, for garnish

fresh mint leaves for garnish

Preparation and cooking time: about 1 hour, plus overnight chilling

Soak the gelatine in cold water. Lightly oil a 1 3/4 pint/1 litre pudding basin with the almond oil. Hull the strawberries and wash them quickly under cold running water. Lay them out to dry on a double layer of kitchen towels. When they are completely dry, process them in a blender with the sugar, then pour the purée into a bowl.

Whip the cream until it is stiff, then gently fold it into the strawberry purée, mixing in with a wooden spoon with an up-and-down movement to prevent the cream from deflating. Heat the Cointreau in a small saucepan until it begins to simmer. Remove from the heat and stir in the gelatine until it has dissolved. Add the desiccated coconut to the strawberry mixture, then slowly pour in the Cointreau and gelatine in a trickle. Mix constantly

with an up-and-down folding movement.

Pour into the basin, bang it gently, cover with cling film and refrigerate overnight. Turn the mousse out on to a serving dish and decorate with the strawberries and the mint leaves. Serve at once.

Strawberry Flan (left) and Strawberry Pillow (above)

Fruit Salad Flan

Crostata alla Macedonia

To serve 6

10 oz/300 g frozen shortcrust pastry

1/2 pint/300 ml milk

pared rind of 1 lemon

3 egg yolks

3 oz/75 g caster sugar

1 oz/25 g flour

butter and flour for the tin and work surface

6 oz/175 g peaches

3 oz/75 g kiwi fruit

2 1/2 oz/70 g banana

2 oz/50 g strawberries

1 1/2 oz/40 g bilberries

1 1/2 oz/40 g raspberries

2 pineapple rings

1 lemon

Preparation and cooking time:
1 hour

Defrost the pastry. Meanwhile, prepare the filling. In a small saucepan, heat the milk with the well-washed and dried lemon rind. In a bowl, beat the yolks with the sugar and sifted flour, then gradually pour on the tepid milk. Return the mixture to the milk pan, and cook, stirring continuously, until the custard thickens. Do not let it boil. Take the custard off the heat and leave to cool at room temperature, stirring occasionally to prevent a skin from forming.

Preheat the oven to 375°F/190°C/gas mark 5. Lightly grease and flour an 8 inch/20 cm flan tin. Flour the work surface and roll out the pastry into a circle large enough to line the base and sides of the tin. Line the base with greaseproof paper and fill with dried baking beans. Bake in the preheated oven for 30 minutes. Remove the beans and paper and leave the flan to cool on a wire rack.

Make the fruit salad only at the last moment, or the fruit will discolour and lose some of their juices. Peel and wash all the fruit, drain and dice or slice into rounds, then place in a bowl. Cover with cling film and refrigerate until ready to use.

When you are ready to serve, fill the flan with the custard and garnish with the fruit.

Mixed Fruit Mélange

Fantasia di Frutta

To serve 2

3 firm, ripe mandarin oranges or clementines

2 kiwi fruits

1 small banana

3 red and 3 green Maraschino cherries

1 tablespoon sugar

juice of 1/2 lemon

2 tablespoons liqueur of your choice

Preparation time: about 30 minutes

Wash and dry the mandarins, then cut them in half crossways. Use a grapefruit knife to loosen the flesh from the skin, without actually removing it. Peel the kiwi fruits and slice them thinly into 16-18 slices. Cut the same number of slices from the banana and finally cut both the red and green cherries in half.

Arrange the six mandarin halves in the centre of 2 small oval-shaped dishes and decorate with the cherries. Put the slices of kiwi fruit round the outside, topped with the banana slices. Leave to rest for a few minutes (do not place in the refrigerator).

Meanwhile, put the sugar in a bowl, add the strained lemon juice and stir until the sugar dissolves. Mix this cold syrup with the liqueur, stir again, pour over the fruit and serve immediately.

Fresh Apricots

Composta di Albicocche

To serve 6

1 1/4 lb/600 g firm ripe apricots

4 oz/100 g apricot jam

1 tablespoon white rum

1 tablespoon apricot liqueur

grated rind of 1 lemon

1 lime for garnish

6 Maraschino cherries

Preparation time: about 15 minutes, plus 1 1/2 hours' soaking

Remove the stalks from the apricots and wipe them with a damp cloth. Halve them, remove the stones and slice them into a basin.

Strain the jam, then dilute it with the rum and liqueur and add the grated lemon rind. Mix well and pour over the apricots, stirring carefully. Cover the basin with cling film and leave in the least cold part of the refrigerator for at least 1 1/2 hours, giving the mixture a gentle stir from time to time.

Serve the apricots in 6 individual bowls. Garnish each one with 5 wafer-thin rings of lime and 5 slices of Maraschino cherry. Serve at once.

Fruit Salad Flan

Summer Fruit Fantasy

Summer Fruit Fantasy

Macedonia Solare

To serve 6

1 large slice ripe watermelon, weighing about 1¹/₄ lb/600 g

2 tablespoons white rum

a small bunch of black grapes

1 oz/25 g sugar

2 tablespoons Cointreau

3 large yellow peaches (not too ripe)

juice of ¹/₂ lemon

fresh mint leaves for garnish

Preparation time: about 1¹/₄ hours

Using a potato scoop or melon-baller, make small, equal-sized balls from the slice of watermelon, discarding any seeds. Place the melon balls in a bowl and sprinkle with the white rum. Cover the bowl with cling film and refrigerate for about 30 minutes.

Wash and dry the grapes, and reserve the best ones. Place the grapes in a small bowl, sprinkle with 1 tablespoon of the sugar and the Cointreau, then set them aside to rest in a cool place for about 15 minutes.

Wash and dry the peaches, cut them into thin slices and drop them into a bowl. Sprinkle with the remaining sugar and the strained lemon juice. Mix gently, cover the bowl and place it in the least cold part of the refrigerator for about 15 minutes.

A short while before serving, arrange the fruit in circles on a large serving dish, garnish with leaves of fresh mint and the reserved grapes, and serve.

September Fruit Salad

Capriccio Settembrino

To serve 4

2 apples

juice of 1 lemon

2 oz/50 g sugar

1 peach

12 oz/350 g Victoria plums

8 oz/250 g green grapes

3 tablespoons Cointreau

Preparation time: about 30 minutes, plus 1 hour chilling

Peel and core the apples, cut into quarters and then dice. As they are diced, drop them into a bowl containing the strained lemon juice. Add the sugar, then mix carefully with a wooden spoon.

Remove the stalks from the peach and the plums and wipe with a damp cloth. Cut in half and remove the stones, then dice them and add them to the apples in the bowl. Wipe the grapes with a damp cloth and remove stalks and pips if necessary. Cut the larger grapes in half. Add to the rest of the fruit. Mix well and pour over the Cointreau.

Cover with cling film and chill for at least 1 hour. Stir gently before serving.

Fruit Cup

Coppa di Frutta

To serve 4

¹/₂ pomegranate

2 tablespoons Cointreau

20 green grapes

1 oz/25 g sugar

juice of ¹/₂ lemon

4 ripe oranges

Preparation time: about 40 minutes

Peel the pomegranate and place the segments in a bowl. Sprinkle with the Cointreau and stir gently. Cover the bowl and place in a cool place. Allow the fruit to soak for about 15 minutes.

Wash and dry the grapes and cut each one lengthwise into 4 segments, taking care to remove the pips. Place the segments in a bowl and dust with the sugar. Sprinkle with the lemon juice, stir and put aside in a cool place for a few minutes.

Peel the oranges, taking care to remove all the pith. Divide the oranges into segments and place in a bowl, squeezing any juice remaining in the peel over them. Add the pomegranate and grape segments, together with their juices, to the orange segments and stir well. Keep in the refrigerator until ready to serve.

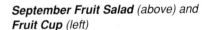

September Fruit Salad (above) and **Fruit Cup** (left)

Zabaglione Trifle

Dolce al Cucchiaio

To serve 10-12

4 eggs, plus 3 yolks

6 oz/175 g caster sugar, plus 1 tablespoon

¹⁄₂ teaspoon vanilla essence

4 oz/100 g flour

salt

butter and flour for the tin and baking tray

2 fl oz/50 ml Marsala wine

3 Golden Delicious apples

³⁄₄ pint/500 ml double cream

3 fl oz/75 ml Maraschino liqueur

juice of 1 lemon

raspberries

Preparation and cooking time: about 2 hours

First make a sponge. Preheat the oven to 375°F/190°C/gas mark 5. Beat the 3 eggs and 4 oz/100 g of the sugar together with the vanilla until light and fluffy. Sift in the flour and a pinch of salt and beat until the mixture makes a smooth batter.

Butter and flour an 8 inch/20 cm cake tin. Spoon in the mixture and bake in the oven for about 35 minutes, or until the cake springs back when lightly pressed with a finger. Turn out the cake and leave to cool on a wire rack. Increase the oven temperature to 475°F/240°C/gas mark 9.

Now prepare the zabaglione. Combine 2 oz/50 g of the caster sugar with the Marsala wine, the remaining egg and egg yolks and a pinch of salt in a stainless steel bowl. Stand the bowl in a bain-marie of tepid water, place over very low heat and whisk the eggs until risen, creamy and thick. Remove from the bain-marie and leave to cool.

Core 2 of the apples, peel and slice thinly, then arrange on a greased baking tray. Sprinkle with 1 tablespoon sugar, then cook in the hot oven for about 5 minutes. Whip the cream and fold about ¹⁄₃ pint/200 ml into the

prepared zabaglione. Dilute the Maraschino liqueur with a little cold water.

Cut the sponge cake into small slices, brush them with the Maraschino, then arrange a few in the bottom of a bowl. Cover with half the zabaglione, and follow with alternate layers of apple, sponge cake, apple and zabaglione. Level the surface carefully.

Thinly slice the remaining apple, without peeling it. Dip the slices in lemon juice, then drain and arrange them around the edge of the trifle. Put the remaining whipped cream in a piping bag with a ridged nozzle and pipe decoratively on to the trifle. Finish the decoration with a couple of dozen raspberries, and keep in the refrigerator until you are ready to serve the trifle.

Little Orange Balls

Bignoline al Fior d'Arancio

To serve 8-10

8 oz/225 g flour

¹⁄₂ teaspoon baking powder

2 oz/50 g sugar

2 tablespoons olive oil

1 tablespoon rum

grated rind of ¹⁄₂ lemon

a pinch of salt

2 eggs, plus 1 egg yolk

vegetable oil for greasing and frying

1 tablespoon orange flower water

5 tablespoons honey

2 oz/50 g candied orange peel

10 blanched almonds

Preparation and cooking time: about 2 hours

Sift the flour and baking powder together. Make a well in the centre and add the sugar, olive oil, rum, lemon rind, salt, eggs and egg yolk. Fold the ingredients into the flour and combine to a firm smooth paste. Divide into small balls about the size

of a hazelnut, place on a lightly oiled sheet of foil and leave to stand for 30 minutes.

Heat plenty of oil in a large deep-frying pan and fry the balls a few at a time. When they are golden brown, drain them on kitchen paper.

Put the orange flower water, and the honey into a large pan. Heat gently and stir until the ingredients have melted. Leave to cool and then add the candied orange peel, the chopped almonds and the prepared profiteroles. Stir well, then mound on to a serving dish. Serve.

Mandarin Orange Trifle

Crema ai Mandarini

To serve 6-8

¹⁄₂ oz/15 g powdered gelatine

4 egg yolks

3 oz/75 g caster sugar

a little vanilla sugar

1 teaspoon cornflour

a pinch of salt

¹⁄₃ pint/200 ml milk

³⁄₄ pint/500 ml double cream

2 oz/50 g trifle sponge cake

4 tablespoons Strega

1 slice tinned pineapple

1 brandied fig

1 small tin mandarin oranges

4 tablespoons orange marmalade

chocolate vermicelli

Preparation and cooking time: about 1 hour, plus 2 hours' refrigeration

Dissolve the gelatine in a little water. Place the egg yolks, sugar, vanilla sugar, cornflour and salt in a saucepan and beat together until smooth. Dilute with the cold milk and half the cream, then bring to the boil, stirring with a small whisk. Remove from the heat, add the gelatine, and leave to cool but not set, stirring frequently.

Cut the sponge cake into ³/₄ inch/ 2 cm cubes. Place in a large bowl or soufflé dish and soak with the Strega. When the custard has cooled, whip the remaining cream until stiff and fold carefully into the custard. Spread the custard over the sponge pieces and refrigerate the bowl for at least 2 hours, or until the custard has set.

Arrange a well-drained pineapple ring and the brandied fig in the centre, and mandarin sections all round, slightly overlapping. Warm the marmalade with a little water, sieve it and use it to brush the fruit and the surface of the dessert; decorate with chocolate vermicelli and serve at once.

Orange Bavarois

Bavarese all'Arancia

To serve 8

¹/₂ oz/12 g leaf gelatine

1 pint/600 ml milk

5 egg yolks

5 oz/150 g caster sugar

3 oranges

¹/₂ teaspoon vanilla essence

3 tablespoons orange liqueur

1 pint/600 ml whipping cream

diced candied mixed fruit

mixed candied citrus fruit

Preparation time: about 1 hour, plus 12 hours' chilling

Soak the gelatine in cold water while you heat the milk. In a bowl, whisk the egg yolks with the sugar, then gradually stir in the hot, but not boiling, milk. Thoroughly wash and grate the rind of 2 oranges, and add to the custard, together with the vanilla. Set over very moderate heat and heat the custard until thickened, stirring continuously, without letting it boil, or it will curdle. Take the custard off the heat. Thoroughly squeeze out the gelatine and add it to the custard, together with the orange liqueur. Mix

well to dissolve the gelatine, then leave the custard to cool at room temperature.

When the custard has just begun to set, whip the cream very stiffly and fold it into the custard. Pour the mixture into a dampened 2¹/₂ pint/ 1.5 litre pint mould and refrigerate for 12 hours.

Just before serving the bavarois, pass the mould over the steam from a pan of boiling water, then invert it on to a plate. Decorate the dessert with the remaining whipped cream, using a piping bag with a fluted nozzle. Pipe on stripes and rosettes, surround it with thin slices cut from the remaining orange, and finish with a little heap of candied fruit in the middle and thin slices of candied citrus fruit around the edge.

Orange Bavarois

Apple Fritters

Fritelle di Mele

To serve 6

1 oz/25 g butter

¼ oz/7 g fresh yeast

2 tablespoons milk, warmed

5 oz/150 g flour

1 oz/25 g cornflour

salt

1 egg, separated

1 tablespoon Calvados

1 oz/25 g caster sugar

about 4 fl oz/100 ml light beer

oil for frying

1 lb/500 g apples, just ripe and not too large

icing or caster sugar

Preparation and cooking time: about 1 hour, plus 2 hours' resting

Melt the butter in a bain-marie and dissolve the yeast in the warm milk. Sift the flour and the cornflour together into a bowl. Make a well in the centre and put in a pinch of salt and the egg yolk, setting aside the white. Pour in the warm melted butter, the Calvados, sugar, dissolved yeast and milk. Using a wooden spoon, combine the ingredients in the centre of the well and when they are mixed together, start to incorporate the flour. Add the beer as the mixture becomes thicker. Finally mix in 2 tablespoons of lukewarm water. Take care not to whisk vigorously, but stir continuously without lifting. Cover the bowl and keep it in a slightly warm place for about 2 hours.

Whisk the reserved egg whites with a pinch of salt and carefully fold them into the batter, with an up-and-down, rather than circular, movement. Heat a deep, heavy pan with plenty of oil. Peel and core the apples and cut them into rings about ¼ inch/ 6 mm thick. Dry them thoroughly between layers of kitchen paper, then dip them, one at a time, into the batter. When the oil is hot, but not boiling, immerse the battered apple rings and fry until they are golden brown on both sides. Drain them on a plate covered with a double layer of kitchen paper. Serve very hot, sprinkled with icing or caster sugar.

Rich Sponge Cake

'Rich' Sponge Cake

Torta 'ricca'

2 egg yolks, size 1

4 oz/100 g caster sugar

a pinch of salt

½ teaspoon vanilla essence

3 oz/75 g flour

butter and flour for the tin

2 tablespoons Maraschino liqueur

4 oz/100g raspberries, plus a few extra for decoration

12 fl oz/350 ml whipping cream

5 oz/150 g cherries

5 oz/150 g medlars

Preparation and cooking time: about 1½ hours

First make a sponge cake. (You can do this several days beforehand and keep it wrapped in clingfilm.) Preheat the oven to 300°-325°F/150°-160°C/

gas mark 2-3. Using an electric or hand-held mixer, whisk the egg yolks with 3 oz/175 g of the sugar and the salt until any mixture which falls off the whisk does not immediately sink into the mixture in the bowl, but rests lightly on the surface. Stir in the vanilla, then sift in the flour from a height and fold them in, working from top to bottom and vice-versa. Grease and flour a round 10 inch/25 cm cake tin, then pour in the sponge mixture. Bake in the preheated oven for about 20 minutes. Check that the sponge is cooked by inserting a wooden toothpick into the centre; the cake is ready when it comes out dry. Remove from the oven, leave in the tin for 5 minutes, then unmould the sponge on to a pastry rack and leave to cool. The cake should be fairly shallow.

To prepare the syrup, boil the remaining sugar with 3 fl oz/75 ml water for 2 minutes, turn off the heat and add the Maraschino liqueur. Leave the syrup to cool.

To assemble the dessert, place the sponge on a serving plate and brush with the cold syrup. Purée the raspberries. Whip the cream very stiffly, reserving about one-third, then mix the rest with the puréed rapsberries. Spread the mixture over the cake and decorate the dessert with all the remaining stoned and sliced fruit. Put the reserved whipped cream into a piping bag with a star nozzle and pipe on swirls of cream.

Fruit Quiche

Quiche alla Frutta

To serve 6

10 oz/300 g flour, plus extra for the work surface and tin

5 oz/150 g butter, plus extra butter and flour for the tin

a pinch of salt

1 lb/450 g red plums

9 oz/250 g apricots

9 oz/250 g cherries

apricot jam

2 tablespoons breadcrumbs

3 eggs

3 tablespoons caster sugar

¼ teaspoon vanilla essence

¼ pint/150 ml milk

¼ pint/150 g whipping cream

Preparation and cooking time:
about 1 hour 15 minutes

First make the pastry. Mix the flour and butter together until they resemble breadcrumbs. Place in a heap on the work surface and make a well in the centre. Pour in 3 fl oz/75 ml cold water and the salt. Knead quickly to form a pastry, then wrap in cling film and leave to rest in the fridge for about 30 minutes.

Meanwhile, wash, drain and stone the fruit. Cut the plums and apricots into wedges and halve the cherries.

Preheat the oven to 425°F/220°C/ gas mark 7. On a floured surface, roll out the pastry to a thickness of ⅛ inch/3 mm and use it to line the base and sides of a greased and floured 10 inch/25 cm quiche tin. Spread on a few spoons of melted apricot jam and sprinkle with the breadcrumbs, then arrange all the fruit attractively on the quiche. Bake in the very hot oven for 10 minutes.

Meanwhile, in a bowl, mix the eggs with the sugar, the vanilla, milk and unwhipped cream. Pour this mixture over the part-baked quiche. Reduce the oven temperature to 350°F/180°C/ gas mark 4 and bake for another 30 minutes. Melt 5 tablespoons apricot jam and brush it over the hot quiche.

Fruit Quiche

Fruit Quiche

ICE CREAM

One of the earliest desserts on record was snow sweetened with honey,
which was eaten by the ancient Romans – so the Italians obviously
had a head start when it comes to ice creams. It is no surprise, then,
that real Italian ice cream, made from fresh fruit, eggs and cream,
is such a treat, so different from its manufactured equivalent. Banish the
thought that ice cream is only for children – it's an adult indulgence, too,
as these recipes show.

Vanilla Ice Cream

Gelato alla Vaniglia

To serve 6

1 pint/600 ml milk

5 oz/150 g sugar

salt

1 small vanilla pod

5 egg yolks

1 egg white

Preparation time: 30 minutes, plus freezing

Heat most of the milk in a saucepan with the sugar, salt and the vanilla pod until almost boiling. Remove from the heat and remove the pod.

Meanwhile, beat the egg yolks then add, little by little, first the reserved cold milk, then the hot, stirring constantly. When the ingredients are well blended, pour the mixture back into the saucepan and heat for about 2 minutes, stirring.

Pour the mixture into a bowl and let it cool, stirring occasionally. Pour it into an ice cream machine, straining it through a fine sieve. Churn until the ice cream starts to become creamy. Whisk the egg white with a pinch of salt and fold it into the ice cream mixture; this helps to make the ice cream smooth and soft. Finish churning the ice cream, then transfer it to a freezerproof bowl and freeze until required.

Baked Peaches with Vanilla Ice Cream

Pesche al Forno con Gelato alla Vaniglia

To serve 8

4 large peaches, about 1³/₄ lb/850 g

6 oz/175 g caster sugar

1 oz/25 g butter

1 fl oz/25 ml Amaretto liqueur

juice of ¹/₂ lemon

14 fl oz/400 ml milk

4 coffee beans

1 vanilla pod

5 egg yolks

4 fl oz/100 ml whipping cream

icing sugar

Preparation time: about 40 minutes, plus freezing

Baked Peaches with Vanilla Ice Cream

Preheat the oven to 400°F/200°C/gas mark 6. Wash and dry the peaches, halve and stone them and arrange in an ovenproof dish. Sprinkle on the 1¹/₂ oz/40 g of the caster sugar, flakes of butter, Amaretto liqueur and the lemon juice. Cover the dish with foil, then bake in the preheated oven for about 20 minutes.

Meanwhile, prepare the ice cream. Heat the milk with the coffee beans and vanilla pod. In a bowl, mix together the egg yolks and remaining sugar, then gradually strain in the hot, but not boiling, milk, pouring it through a fine sieve. Pour the custard back into the pan and heat very gently until thickened; do not let it boil.

Take the pan off the heat and leave the custard to cool before pouring it into an ice cream maker. Churn until the ice cream becomes creamy, then stir in the lightly whipped cream and finish churning. Transfer the ice cream to a freezerproof bowl and freeze until required.

Scoop out balls of ice cream and arrange them among the cold, baked peaches. Dust with icing sugar and serve.

Coconut Ice Cream with Candied Pineapple

Gelato al Cocco con Ananas Caramellato

To serve 6

2 fl oz/50 ml milk

2 oz/50 g caster sugar, plus a little extra for the pineapple purée

2 fl oz/50 ml double cream

1 teaspoon vanilla essence

¹/₄ pint/150 ml coconut milk

a glass of rum, plus a dash extra for flambéeing

1 large pineapple

butter

a pinch of cornflour

blackcurrants

Preparation time: about 40 minutes, plus freezing

To make the ice cream, heat, but do not boil, the milk with the sugar, cream and half the vanilla. Take the pan off the heat and add the coconut milk and the rum. Leave to cool, then pour the mixture into an ice cream maker and churn according to the instructions. As soon as the ice cream is ready, transfer it to a freezerproof bowl and freeze until required.

Shortly before serving, peel and core the pineapple and cut 6 even slices, about ¹/₂ inch/1 cm thick, from the middle of the fruit. Purée the remainder with 4 fl oz/100 ml cold water and a spoonful of sugar. Sieve the purée and set aside.

Dry the pineapple slices and brown them over high heat with a nut of butter, then remove them from the pan and flambé the cooking juices with a dash of rum. As soon as the alcohol has evaporated, add the cornflour slaked with a drop of water and the reserved pineapple purée. Cook over a moderate heat until the sauce has thickened, then turn off the heat, whisk in a nut of butter and flavour with the remaining vanilla.

Arrange the pineapple slices and scoops of ice cream on a plate, pour the sauce all over and decorate with clusters of blackcurrants.

Coconut Ice Cream with Candied Pineapple

Coffee Ice Cream

Gelato al Caffè

To serve 6

2 oz/50 g coffee

1 sachet of vanilla sugar

12 oz/350 g sugar

⅓ pint/200 ml single cream

1 egg white

a pinch of salt

Preparation time: 30 minutes, plus chilling and freezing

In a small saucepan, bring 12 fl oz/ 350 ml of water to the boil, pour in the coffee and, stirring constantly, simmer over very low heat until the foam has disappeared. Leave to infuse for about 15 minutes, so that the ground coffee sinks to the bottom of the saucepan; strain the liquid coffee into a bowl.

Add the vanilla sugar and the sugar and stir until the sugars dissolve then leave to cool. At this point mix in the cream and place in the refrigerator for at least 1 hour to cool completely.

Pour the mixture into an ice cream maker. Add the egg white whisked to a froth with the salt, so that the ice cream will be smooth and soft. Churn according to the instructions. Transfer to a freezerproof bowl and freeze until required.

Lemon Ice Cream with Strawberry Coulis

Gellato Rosato

To serve 4

1 lb/450 g lemon ice cream

8 oz/225 g fresh strawberries

3 tablespoons Cointreau

1 oz/25 g sugar

8 wafers

Preparation time: about 15 minutes, plus 2 hours' soaking

Keep the ice cream in the freezer for at least 2 hours before preparation.

Meanwhile, rinse the strawberries in iced water, drain well and discard the hulls. Cut the strawberries into pieces and place them in a bowl. Pour on the Cointreau and sprinkle with the sugar. Cover the bowl and leave to soak for a couple of hours.

Just before you are ready to serve, purée the strawberries with their syrup to form a smooth sauce. Remove the ice cream from the freezer and, using a scoop, place balls of the ice cream either in a large serving goblet or in individual glasses. Coat the ice cream with the strawberry sauce and serve with the wafers.

Lemon Ice Cream with Strawberry Coulis

Pistachio Ice Cream

Gelato al Pistachio

To serve 6

4 oz/100 g pistachio nuts

a pinch of salt

8 oz/225 g sugar

1 pint/600 ml milk

1 vanilla pod

5 egg yolks

Preparation time: 30 minutes, plus freezing

Plunge the pistachio nuts into salted boiling water for 1 minute, then drain and shell them. Pound them in a mortar, adding 1 tablespoon of the sugar from time to time, until they are reduced to powder.

Heat most of the milk with the remaining sugar and the vanilla pod and bring slowly to the boil, stirring occasionally with a wooden spoon. Remove from the heat and discard the pod.

Meanwhile, beat the egg yolks in a bowl with the powdered pistachio nuts, using a small whisk to obtain a smooth mixture. Add first the reserved cold milk, then the hot, stirring constantly. When the ingredients are well blended, pour the mixture back into the saucepan and heat for about 2 minutes, stirring. Pour the mixture into a bowl and let it cool, stirring occasionally.

Pour into an ice cream machine, straining it through a fine sieve, and churn according to the instructions. When the ice cream is creamy, transfer to a freezerproof bowl and freeze until required.

Amaretto Ice Cream

Gelato all'Amaretto

To serve 6

1 pint/600 ml milk

1 vanilla pod

5 egg yolks

a pinch of salt

5oz/150 g sugar

4 oz/100g Amaretti biscuits

4 tablespoons Amaretto liqueur

Preparation and cooking time: 1¹/₂ hours, plus freezing

Heat the milk in a saucepan with the vanilla pod and bring slowly to the boil. Strain, remove from the heat and remove the pod. Leave to cool.

Meanwhile, beat the egg yolks with the salt and sugar until soft and frothy. Stir in the tepid milk, pouring it in a trickle, then whisk until well blended. Pour the mixture back into the saucepan, place over a very low heat and heat, stirring constantly, until the mixture is about to boil.

Remove from the heat and strain the liquid through a fine sieve, then leave to cool at room temperature, stirring occasionally. Add the finely crumbled Amaretti biscuits and Amaretto liqueur. Place in the refrigerator for about 1 hour, then pour the mixture into an ice cream maker. Churn, following the instructions. When the ice cream is creamy, transfer it to a freezerproof bowl and freeze until required.

Ice Cream Cake

Torta Gelato

To serve 8

2 pints/1.2 litres milk

3 eggs, plus 4 egg yolks

18 oz/500 g caster sugar

1 teaspoon vanilla essence

14 oz/400 g peaches, peeled and stoned, plus extra for decorating

4 oz/100 g flour

butter and flour for the cake tin

$^{1}/_{3}$ glass Alchermes or Maraschino liqueur

5 oz/150 g cherry jam

2 peaches, sliced

$^{1}/_{3}$ pint/200 g whipping cream, whipped

1 banana, sliced

Preparation time: about 1 hour, plus freezing

1) To make the vanilla ice cream, heat 1 pint/600 ml of the milk. In a bowl, beat the egg yolks with 5 oz/150 g of the sugar and $^{1}/_{4}$ teaspoon of the vanilla, then gradually pour in the hot milk. Return the custard to the milk pan and simmer over very low heat for a few minutes, stirring continuously. Do not let it boil.

2) Pour the custard into an ice cream maker and churn according to the instructions. When the ice cream is creamy, transfer it to a freezerproof bowl and freeze until required.

To make the peach ice cream, purée half the peaches with the remaining 1 pint/600 ml milk and 9 oz/250 g of the sugar. Churn in the ice cream maker, then freeze.

3) Now make a sponge cake for the base. Preheat the oven to 350°F/180°C/gas mark 4. Whisk the eggs with the remaining 4 oz/100 g caster sugar to a ribbon consistency. Stir in the remaining vanilla, then sift in the flour from a height and fold in. Grease

and flour a round 8$^{1}/_{2}$ inch/22 cm cake tin and spoon in the sponge mixture. Bake in the preheated oven for about 35 minutes. Remove from the oven and leave to cool on a wire rack.

4) Blend the liqueur with the cherry jam and 2 tablespoons cold water. Split the sponge cake horizontally into 3 layers and brush each with the jam mixture.

5) Line the base of a 9 inch/23 cm springform cake tin with greaseproof paper. Line the edge with a $^{3}/_{4}$ inch/2 cm strip of sponge cake.

6) Fill the mould with half the peach ice cream, cover with peach slices, then make a layer of all the vanilla ice cream and finish with the remaining peach ice cream. Cover the top securely with thick foil and place the cake in the freezer.

To serve, remove cake from freezer and let stand for 5-10 minutes. Remove the foil and unmould on to a serving plate, easing away the sides of the cake tin with a palette knife. Decorate with whipped cream and sliced banana and peaches.

1

2

3

4

5

6

Tri-colour Ice Cream Tart

Torta Gelato Tricolore

To serve 8

4¹/₂ oz/125 g fresh apricot pulp

18 fl oz/500 ml milk

11 oz/325 g caster sugar

6 fl oz/175 ml whipping cream

4¹/₂ oz/125 g raspberries

1 vanilla pod

2 egg yolks

3 eggs

4 oz/100 g sugar

a pinch of salt

¹/₂ teaspoon vanilla essence

4 oz/100 g flour

butter and flour for the baking sheet

fresh fruit for decoration

Preparation and cooking time: about 1 hour, plus freezing

The ice creams can be prepared a day in advance. For the apricot ice cream, blend the pulp with ¹/₄ pint/ 150 ml of the milk, 4¹/₂ oz/125 g of the sugar and half the unwhipped cream for about 1 minute. Pour into an ice cream maker and churn according to the instructions. As soon as the ice cream is creamy, transfer it to a freezerproof bowl and place in the freezer. Make the raspberry ice cream in the same way, using the raspberries, ¹/₄ pint/150 ml of the milk, 4¹/₄ oz/125 g of the caster sugar and 3 fl oz/75 ml of the unwhipped cream, then freeze it.

To make the vanilla ice cream, heat the remaining 8 fl oz/225 ml milk with the vanilla pod. Meanwhile, mix the egg yolks with the remaining sugar. Gradually pour on the strained hot milk, then return the custard to the milk pan and cook until thickened, but do not boil. Leave the custard to cool, then pour it into an ice cream maker and churn according to the instructions.

As soon as it is ready, transfer it to a springform cake pan, and freeze until solid.

Spread the raspberry ice cream over the vanilla and finally the apricot ice cream, then level the surface.

Cover the top securely with thick foil, and keep in the freezer until ready to serve.

To make a sponge base, whisk the eggs with the sugar and the salt and the vanilla until puffed up and light, then fold in the flour. Spoon the mixture on to a greased 8¹/₂ inch/22 cm long baking sheet lined with a sheet of greased and floured greaseproof paper, then bake in the preheated oven for about 15 minutes. Remove from the oven, peel the sponge off the paper and, when it is cool, cut out a circle the same diameter as the springform tin. Unmould the ice cream on to the sponge, garnish with slices of fresh fruit, then serve.

Nougat Ice Cream

Gelato al Torroncino

To serve 6

5 oz/150 g assorted crystallized fruit

2 fl oz/50 ml Maraschino liqueur

4 oz/100 g Italian nougat (torrone)

1 pint/600 ml milk

1 vanilla pod

7 oz/200 g sugar

4 egg yolks

Preparation and cooking time: 1¹/₂ hours, plus freezing

Coarsely chop the crystallized fruit, of different colours and flavours, then place it in a small bowl and moisten it with the Maraschino liqueur. Pound the nougat to a powder.

In a saucepan, heat most of the milk with the vanilla pod and the sugar. When the milk is hot and the sugar has dissolved, discard the pod.

Beat the egg yolks in a bowl adding first the reserved cold milk then the hot, pouring it in a trickle and stirring constantly. When all the ingredients are well mixed, pour them back into the saucepan and heat for a couple of minutes, stirring, without bringing it to the boil. Remove the saucepan from the heat and strain the mixture into a bowl. Let it cool, stirring occasionally, then leave it for at least 1 hour in the refrigerator.

Just before placing it in an ice-cream machine, mix in the crystallized

fruit and the nougat. Churn according to the instructions, then transfer to a freezerproof bowl and freeze until required.

Pear Ice Cream with Fruits of the Forest Sauce

Gelato di Pere con Salsa ai Frutti di Bosco

To serve 6

14 oz/400 g pears

7 oz/200 g caster sugar

18 fl oz/500 ml milk

5 oz/150 g bilberries

5 oz/150 g raspberries

4 oz/100 g blackcurrants

3 fl oz/75 ml Grappa

langue de chat **biscuits**

Preparation time: about 30 minutes, plus freezing and macerating

First make the ice cream. Peel and core the pears, then dice them and place in a blender or food processor. Add 5 oz/150 g of the sugar and the milk and blend at maximum speed for 1 minute, then pour the mixture into an ice cream maker and churn according to the instructions. When the ice cream is creamy, transfer it to a freezerproof bowl and freeze until required.

To make the sauce, wash the fruit and drain well, then place them in a bowl with the remaining 2 oz/50 g sugar and the Grappa. Cover with cling film and leave to macerate in the fridge for at least 6 hours.

When you are ready to serve the ice cream, scoop it into 6 appropriate coupes and pour over the fruit sauce. Finish with some *langue de chat* biscuits and serve immediately.

Tri-colour Ice Cream Tart (left) and Pear Ice Cream with Fruits of the Forest Sauce (above)

Greedy Nests

Nidi Golosi

To serve 8

5 oz/150 g egg whites

1¼ lb/600 g caster sugar

a pinch of salt

½ teaspoon vanilla essence

butter and flour for the baking sheet

10 oz/300 g puréed peach pulp

1 pint/600 ml whipping cream

1½ pints/900 ml milk

10 oz/300 g raspberries

14 oz/400 g peaches

7 oz/200 g raspberries

fresh mint

Preparation and cooking time: about 3½ hours

First make the meringue. (This can be done several days in advance.) Preheat the oven to 140°F/60°C/gas low. Put the egg whites with 10 oz/300 g of the sugar and the salt in a bowl and stand the base in a tepid bain-marie. Beat until very firm, then add the vanilla. Put the meringue into a piping bag with a fluted nozzle and pipe out 8 large nests on to a greased and floured baking sheet. Bake in the warm oven for about 3 hours, making sure that the nests are completely dry before removing them from the oven.

To make the peach ice cream, blend the peach pulp for 1 minute with ¼ pint/150 ml of the unwhipped cream, 5 oz/150 g of the caster sugar and ¾ pint/450 ml of milk. Churn in an ice cream maker according to the instructions. As soon as the ice cream is creamy, transfer it to a freezerproof bowl and freeze. Make the raspberry ice cream in the same way, using the raspberries, ¼ pint/150 ml unwhipped whipping cream, 5 oz/150 g caster sugar and ¾ pint/450 ml milk.

To assemble the nests, whip the remaining whipping cream and divide it between the nests. Fill with balls of mixed ice cream and decorate with sliced peaches, raspberries and sprigs of mint.

Orange Sorbet

Sorbetto all'Arancia

To serve 8

juice of 6 or 7 juicy oranges (reserve the shells)

grated rind of 2 oranges

14 oz/400 g caster sugar, plus 2 tablespoons

1 egg white

a pinch of salt

1 oz/25 g pistachios, blanched, skinned and chopped

biscuits, to serve

Preparation time: about 30 minutes, plus freezing

Clean 8 orange shell halves, scraping out the internal membrane, then place them in the freezer. Strain the orange juice into a bowl. Mix in the grated rind and 14 oz/400 g sugar. Refrigerate the juice for about 2 hours, stirring frequently to dissolve all the sugar. Transfer the mixture to an ice cream maker and churn according to the instructions.

Meanwhile, beat the egg white with the salt until very firm, then fold in 2 tablespoons sugar. As soon as the orange juice mixture begins to firm up, stop churning for a moment and add half the beaten egg white (discard the remaining beaten egg white). Start the machine again and finish churning the sorbet. Place the sorbet in the freezer; the egg white will keep it soft.

Just before serving, take the orange shells out of the freezer and cut a sliver off the bases so that they stand firmly. Fill with the sorbet, sprinkle with chopped pistachios and serve with little biscuits.

Greedy Nests (left), Orange Sorbet (above right) and *Charlotte Meringue with Mandarin Sorbet (right)*

Charlotte Meringue with Mandarin Sorbet

Charlotte Meringata al Sorbetto di Mandarino

To serve 8

¹/₄ **pint/150 ml mandarin juice, plus the peel from the squeezed fruit**

8 oz/225 g caster sugar, plus 1 tablespoon extra

5 egg whites

1 x 7 inch/17.5 cm sponge cake

3 fl oz/75 ml Grand Marnier

10 oz/300 g strawberries

¹/₄ **fresh pineapple, freshly diced**

a pinch of salt

Preparation and cooking time: about 2 hours

Steep the mandarin peel overnight in the juice, 4 oz/100 g sugar and ¹/₄ pint/150 ml water.

Next day, strain the infusion and churn in an ice cream maker, following the instructions. As soon as it begins to solidify, add one-third of the egg white beaten with the remaining 1 tablespoon sugar, and finish churning (discard the remaining beaten egg white). Transfer the sorbet to the freezer.

Slice the cake lengthways into ¹/₂ inch/1 cm slices. Cut 5 or 6 of the longest into rectangles as long as the diameter of your mould; halve them into equal triangles and arrange them like rays in the mould, the points converging in the centre. Line the sides with some of the remaining slices, cutting off the excess.

Brush the lining sponge with Grand Marnier diluted with a little water. Fill the mould with the strawberries, pineapple and sorbet, alternating the layers with the remaining cake. Chill in the freezer for at least 4 hours.

Preheat the oven to 475°F/240°C/ gas mark 9. Just before serving, beat the remaining 4 egg whites with the salt until very firm, adding the remaining sugar little by little.

Unmould the charlotte on to an ovenproof plate and cover it with this meringue, then bake in the hot oven for not more than 3-4 minutes. Serve immediately.

Ice Cream Sponge with Forest Fruits

Biscotto Gelato ai Frutti di Bosco

To serve 8

4 eggs, plus 5 extra yolks

15 oz/450 g caster sugar

5 oz/150 g flour

3 tablespoons cocoa powder

butter for greasing the tin

1 pint/600 ml milk

1 vanilla pod

12 fl oz/350 ml whipping cream

7 oz/200 g mixed forest fruits

Cointreau

Preparation and cooking time:
about 1 hour, plus freezing

1) Preheat the oven to 350°F/180°C/ gas mark 4. First make the sponge. In an electric mixer, whisk the eggs with 5 oz/150 g of the sugar, then sift in the flour and cocoa from a height. Grease a 16 x 13½ inch/40 x 34 cm baking tray, cover with a sheet of greased greaseproof paper and pour on the sponge mixture, levelling it with a palette knife. Bake in the preheated oven for 8 minutes, then remove and invert the sponge on to a tea towel.

2) To make the ice cream, heat the milk with 7 oz/200 g of the sugar and the vanilla pod. Cool, strain, add ½ pint/300 ml of the cream, whisk well and pour into an ice cream maker. Churn according to the instructions.

3) Macerate half the fruit in 5 tablespooons Cointreau. Place the rest in a saucepan with the remaining sugar, the egg yolks and 2 tablespoons Cointreau. Whisk together over moderate heat until smooth and creamy. Cool, then add the macerated fruit and 2 fl oz/50 ml whipped cream.

4) Trim the edges of the sponge and use it to line the base and sides of a 1¼ pint/750 ml mould. Brush lightly with Cointreau.

5) Fill the mould with the ice cream, making a deep hollow in the centre.

6) Fill up with the fruit and cream mixture, then cover the top with the sponge trimmings. Freeze for about 4 hours. Serve the ice cream sponge with fresh fruit.

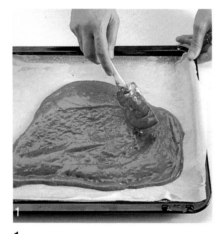

1

2

3

4

5

6

Winter Melon Sorbet

Sorbetto al Melone d'Inverno

To serve 4

6 oz/175 g caster sugar

rind of 1 lemon, cut into strips

10 oz/300 g pale green melon pulp

vodka

1 egg white, lightly beaten

pomegranate seeds

lime slices

pale green winter melon slices

Preparation time: about 10 minutes, plus freezing

Boil the sugar with 9 fl oz/250 ml water and lemon rind for 2 minutes; strain this syrup and leave to cool.

Meanwhile, purée the melon pulp in a blender or food processor and add it to the cold syrup. Add a glass of vodka, then churn the mixture in an ice cream maker, following the instructions. As soon as the sorbet begins to thicken, add the egg white and finish churning the sorbet (about 20 minutes in total).

Transfer the sorbet to a freezer-proof container and freeze. Serve scooped into balls like ice cream. Garnish with pomegranate seeds, slices of lime and slivers of melon.

Iced Lemons with Lemon and Raspberry Sorbets

Cedri Ghiacciati

To serve 6

4 large lemons

1lb 2 oz/500 g caster sugar

9 oz/250 g fresh raspberries, plus a few for decoration

1 fl oz/25 ml rum

Preparation time: about 1 hour, plus overnight infusing

First make the lemon sorbet, beginning a day ahead. Thoroughly wash the 3 largest lemons and halve them vertically. Scrape out the pulp and juice into a bowl. Refrigerate the empty lemon shells. Mix together half the sugar, 14 fl oz/400 ml water and the pared rind of a quarter lemon and leave in the fridge to infuse overnight.

Strain the infusion and add the lemon juice and pulp, then pour into an ice cream maker and churn according to the instructions. Transfer the sorbet to a freezerproof bowl and freeze as soon as it is ready.

To make the raspberry sorbet, purée the raspberries with 9 oz/250 g of the sugar, the rum and 14 fl oz/400 ml water. Transfer to the ice cream maker and churn, then place the sorbet in the freezerproof bowl and freeze.

Just before serving, fill the lemon shells with a portion of both sorbets and decorate with fresh raspberries.

Coffee Sorbet in Pastry Baskets

Sorbetto al Caffè in Coupelle

To serve 8

---

14 oz/400 g sugar

---

9 fl oz/250 ml very strong black coffee

---

3 egg whites, size 2

---

2 oz/50 g flour

---

2 oz/50 g butter, melted and cooled, plus extra for greasing baking sheet

---

2 oz/50 g icing sugar

Preparation and cooking time: about 1 hour, plus freezing

First make the coffee sorbet. Boil 12 oz/350 g sugar with 9 fl oz/250 ml water for 1 minute, then add the coffee to this syrup. Mix together and leave to cool. Pour the coffee syrup into an ice cream maker and churn according to the instructions.

Meanwhile, beat 2 of the egg whites with the remaining sugar until very firm. As soon as the sorbet begins to solidify, add ½ tablespoon of beaten egg white and finish churning. Transfer the sorbet to a freezerproof bowl and freeze.

To make the pastry baskets, preheat the oven to 425°F/220°C/gas mark 7. In a bowl, combine the flour, cooled melted butter, icing sugar and remaining unbeaten egg whites and work with a small whisk to obtain a soft paste. Brush a baking sheet with butter, cover with a sheet of greaseproof paper and grease this as well. Put on a small spoonful of paste, flatten it with the back of a spoon to make a very thin disc, about 6 inches/15 cm across. Make at least 7 more discs in this way, spacing them well apart as they will spread during baking.

Bake in the hot oven for a few minutes, until they are pale in the centre, but browned at the edges. Lift them off the paper with a palette knife (they should be soft and malleable), then mould them into baskets over the base of an up-turned cup. Lift off the baskets when they are cold.

Just before serving, fill the baskets with scoops of the sorbet and immediately take the dessert to the table.

Iced Lemons with Lemon and Raspberry Sorbets (left) and Coffee Sorbet in Pastry Baskets (below)

Pastry Baskets with Ice Cream and Rhubarb Compôte

Coupelle Congelato e Composta Dirabarbo

To serve 6

2 oz/50 g flour

2 egg whites, size 2

2 oz/50 g icing sugar

2 oz/50 g butter, melted and cooled, plus extra for greasing

1 lb 2 oz/500 g rhubarb

1 Golden Delicious apple

1 oz/25 g butter

2 tablespoons caster sugar

vanilla ice cream, to serve

fresh mint, to decorate

Preparation and cooking time: about 1 hour

First make the pastry baskets. (The baskets can be prepared a day in advance and kept in a cool, dry place.) Preheat the oven to 400°F/ 200°C/gas mark 6. In a bowl, mix the flour with the unbeaten egg whites, the sugar and cold melted butter. Stir very gently, then place a spoonful of the mixture on a greased baking sheet lined with a sheet of greased greaseproof paper. Flatten the little heap with the back of a spoon to make a thin 4 inch/10 cm disc. Make at least 5 more discs in the same way, spacing them well apart.

Bake in the hot oven for 3 - 4 minutes, until the discs are browned at the edges but still pale in the centre. Carefully lift them off the baking sheet and, while they are still malleable, mould them over the base of an up-turned cup or glass to make basket shapes. Make at least 6 baskets.

Trim the rhubarb and peel away the tough fibres with a potato peeler, then cut into chunks. Cut the apple into wedges. Heat the butter until

Pastry Baskets with Ice Cream and Rhubarb Compôte and Pineapple Sorbet in Strawberry Sauce

foaming, then brown the rhubarb and apple over high heat. Sprinkle with the caster sugar and cook until well coated.

Place 2 scoops of ice cream in each pastry basket, decorate with fresh mint leaves and serve on individual plates accompanied by the rhubarb compôte.

Pineapple Sorbet in Strawberry and Rabspberry Sauce

Sorbetto di Ananas Affogato

To serve 6

12 oz/350 g fresh pineapple pulp, plus 2 large rings for decoration

15 oz/450 g caster sugar

1 egg white

7 oz/200 g strawberries

4 oz/100 g raspberries

1 fl oz/25 ml Cointreau

Preparation time: about 30 minutes, plus freezing

To make the sorbet, purée the pineapple pulp with 10 oz/300 g of the sugar and 1/2 pint/300 ml water. Transfer to an ice cream maker and churn according to the instructions. When the sorbet starts to become firm and thick, add 1 tablespoon of stiffly beaten egg white (discard the remaining beaten egg white) and finish churning. Transfer the sorbet to a freezerproof bowl and freeze until ready to serve.

To make the sauce, purée the strawberries and raspberries with the remaining sugar, the Cointreau and 3 fl oz/75 ml cold water.

Scoop out small balls of sorbet with an ice cream scoop and place in serving bowls. Add 2 pineapple wedges cut from the rings to each bowl and smother with the fruit sauce.

Strawberry Ice Cream with Meringues

Strawberry Ice Cream with Meringues

Gelata alla Meringa

To serve 6

8 oz/250 g strawberries

12 oz/350 g caster sugar

18 fl oz/500 ml milk

4 egg whites, size 2

1/4 teaspoon vanilla essence

butter for greasing

vanilla-flavoured custard

Preparation and cooking time: about 40 minutes, plus freezing the ice cream and baking the meringues

First make the ice cream. (This can be done several days in advance.) Hull, carefully wash and thoroughly drain the strawberries, then place them in the goblet of a blender with

5 oz/150 g of the sugar and the milk. Blend on full power for 2 minutes, then transfer to an ice cream maker and churn following the instructions. When the ice cream is creamy, transfer it to a freezerproof bowl and freeze.

You can also prepare the meringues in advance. Preheat the oven to 300°F/150°C/gas mark 2. Put the egg whites, the remaining sugar and vanilla in a bowl. Stand the bowl in a pan containing two fingers of tepid water, place over very low heat and beat the egg whites with a whisk or an electric beater until very stiff.

Place the meringue in a piping bag fitted with a plain nozzle. Grease a baking tray, then pipe walnut-sized meringues on to it, spaced well apart. Bake in the preheated oven for about 3 hours, until the meringues are firm and crisp; they should be white and perfectly dry. If they begin to brown, prop the oven door open a little.

To serve, place 3 or 4 scoops of ice cream in each dish, together with 3 or 4 meringues. Serve with vanilla-flavoured custard.

CHOCOLATE

There's nothing more sinful, more mind-blastingly delicious than chocolate. It's so glorious that many people are addicted to it. If that applies to you, you'll be in absolute heaven throughout this chapter. So go on, spoil yourself – just this once, or twice ...

Chocolate Puff Pastry Tart

Sfogliata di Cioccolato

To serve 8

10 oz/300 g frozen puff pastry

2 oz/50 g butter, melted and cooled, plus extra for greasing the tin

3 eggs

5 oz/150 g caster sugar

1/2 teaspoon vanilla essence

a pinch of salt

4 fl oz/100 ml milk, at room temperature

3 oz/75 g dark chocolate

4 oz/100 g pine nuts

2 sponge fingers, finely crumbled

4 fl oz/125 ml whipping cream

icing sugar

2 Amaretti biscuits, finely crumbled

Preparation and cooking time:
1 hour 15 minutes, plus defrosting the pastry

Defrost the pastry according to the instructions on the packet. Grease a plain 11 inch/28 cm tart tin. Whisk the eggs with the sugar, vanilla and salt, then gradually pour in the milk and tepid melted butter.

Break up the chocolate and melt it in a bain-marie or over very low heat, then stir it into the egg mixture.

Pound the pine nuts in a mortar, or whizz briefly in a food processor, and add them to the mixture, whisking continuously with an electric mixer.

Preheat the oven to 350°F/180°C/gas mark 4. Roll out the pastry into a circle large enough to line the base and sides of the tart tin. Prick the bottom with a fork and sprinkle with the crumbled sponge fingers. Pour in the chocolate mixture, spreading it evenly and bake the tart on the lowest shelf of the preheated oven (to ensure that the pastry on the bottom is thoroughly baked) for 45 minutes.

Unmould the tart on to a wire rack and leave to cool.

Whip the cream until very stiff and put into a piping bag with a star nozzle. Sift icing sugar over all the cooled tart except in the centre, then pipe rosettes of cream into the centre and round the edge of the tart. Sprinkle the rosettes with crumbled Amaretti biscuits and serve the tart immediately.

Zabaglione Coupes with Sweet White Wine

Coppe di Sabaione al Vino Bianco

To serve 8

3 eggs, plus 8 yolks

7 oz/200 g caster sugar

3 oz/75 g flour

3 tablespoons cocoa powder

a pinch of salt

butter and flour for the tin

icing sugar

3 fl oz/75 ml Kirsch

7 oz/200 g plain chocolate

18 fl oz/500 ml double cream

1/3 pint/200 ml dessert white wine

fresh raspberries, for decoration

Preparation and cooking time: about 2 1/2 hours

Preheat the oven to 350°F/180°C/ gas mark 4. To make the chocolate sponge, beat 2 eggs and 3 oz/75 g sugar together until they are light and fluffy. Carefully sprinkle on the sieved flour, cocoa and salt to colour and flavour it and continue beating until the mixture forms a smooth batter.

Butter and flour an 9 inch/23 cm long Swiss roll tin and spoon in the batter, smoothing the top. Bake in the oven for 10-15 minutes until it comes away slightly from the edges of the tin and the cake springs back slightly when pushed with a finger. Set aside to cool, then transfer to a piece of non-stick paper dusted with icing sugar. Brush the sponge with a mixture of Kirsch and cold water.

Melt the chocolate over gentle heat with the 4 fl oz/100 ml of cream, then spread this over the sponge. Using the non-stick paper, roll up like a Swiss roll, starting from one of the longer sides.

Just before assembling the coupes, make the zabaglione. Combine the remaining whole egg, 8 yolks, 4 oz/100 g sugar and wine in a bowl, and stand it in a hot bain-marie over very moderate heat. Beat until the zabaglione is foamy; leave to cool. Whip the remaining 14 fl oz/400 ml cream and fold it into the cool zabaglione.

Divide the zabaglione between 8 dishes. Slice the sponge into rounds and garnish the zabaglione with these. Top with fresh raspberries.

Chocolate Mousse

Crema all'Amaretto

To serve 6-8

9 oz /250 g plain chocolate

4 oz/100 g Amaretti biscuits

4 egg yolks

4 oz/100 g sugar

3 oz/75 g flour

1 3/4 pints/1 litre milk

1/2 teaspoon vanilla essence

2 oz/50 g butter, cut into small pieces

2-3 tablespoons Amaretto liqueur

2 oz/50 g flaked almonds

Preparation and cooking time: about 50 minutes

Grate the chocolate and finely crush the Amaretti biscuits. Whisk the egg yolks with the sugar until they form soft, whitish peaks. Fold in the sifted flour and 2 tablespoons of cold milk and stir until the mixture is smooth and free of lumps. Add the remaining milk and the vanilla.

Gently heat the mixture in a saucepan and bring it just to the boil, stirring constantly with a whisk. Cook for a few minutes, remove from the heat and stir in the butter, grated

chocolate and crushed biscuits.

Pour the Amaretto liqueur into a serving bowl, making sure that the sides of the bowl are coated in the liqueur.

Pour in the prepared mixture and leave to cool. Top with the flaked almonds, cover with cling film and keep in the refrigerator until ready to serve.

Chocolate Puff Pastry Tart

Chocolate and Meringue Caskets

Cofanetti di Meringa al Cioccolato

To serve 8

6¹/₂ oz/185 g caster sugar

3 egg whites, size 2

a pinch of salt

butter and flour for the baking sheets

4 fl oz/100 ml whipping cream

1 tablespoon rum

11 oz/325 g plain chocolate

10 oz/300 g icing sugar

1 tablespoon lemon juice

Preparation and cooking time: about 1 hour 20 minutes, plus baking the meringues

First prepare the meringues. (This can be done the day before.) Preheat the oven to 120°F/50°C/gas low.

Heat 1 fl oz/25 ml water with 5 oz/150 g sugar over a moderate heat until the syrup reaches 239°F/115°C on a sugar thermometer. Immediately take the pan off the heat and immerse it in cold water to prevent further cooking.

Meanwhile, beat the egg whites with the remaining sugar and salt until very stiff. Then, whisking continuously, pour in the syrup in a thin stream to make a homogenous mass. Put it into a piping bag with a plain nozzle and pipe plum-sized balls on to several greased and floured baking sheets. Bake in the preheated oven for about 4 hours, then turn off the heat and leave the meringues to cool in the oven until completely cold.

Just before serving, prepare the chocolate cream. Heat the unwhipped cream with the rum in a bain-marie, then chop and add 9 oz/250 g of the chocolate. As soon as it has melted, remove the mixture from the bain-marie and beat with a wire whisk to obtain a smooth cream. Delicately scrape the base of the meringues to make a small cavity. Pipe in the chocolate cream, using a piping bag with a fine plain nozzle.

Cover a baking tray with a sheet of greaseproof paper, arrange the meringues on it and chill in the fridge for about 1 hour so that the cream hardens and does not seep out of the little 'caskets'.

Meanwhile, make the icing. Sift the icing sugar, then beat it slowly with the lemon juice and a few drops of cold water into a smooth paste. Place in a piping cone. Remove the meringues from the fridge, arrange them on a pastry rack set over a large tray (to catch the drips) and coat with icing. Leave to harden. While that is happening, melt the remaining chocolate in a bain-marie and place in a piping cone. Decorate each meringue with a line of chocolate and serve in paper cases.

Chocolate Meringue Tart

Crostata di Cioccolato Meringata

To serve 8

5 oz/150 g butter, softened and diced, plus extra for the tin

5 oz/150 g flour

5 egg yolks

4 oz/100 g cornflour

4 oz/100 g icing sugar

¹/₂ teaspoon vanilla essence

salt

6¹/₂ oz/185 g caster sugar, plus 1 tablespoon for the almonds

³/₄ oz/20 g flour

9 fl oz/250 ml milk, hot

5 oz/150 g plain chocolate, chopped

2 tablespoons Grand Marnier

5 egg whites

3 oz/75 g almonds, finely chopped

Preparation and cooking time: about 1 hour 15 minutes

To make the pastry, work the diced butter with the flour until the mixture resembles breadcrumbs, then place on the work surface and make a well in the centre. Put in 3 egg yolks, the cornflour, icing sugar, vanilla and a pinch of salt. Knead quickly with your fingertips, then wrap the pastry in cling film and leave to rest in the fridge for about 30 minutes.

Meanwhile, prepare the filling. In a small saucepan, mix 2 egg yolks with 1½ oz/40 g of the sugar and the flour, then gradually stir in the hot milk. Set over moderate heat and simmer for 5 minutes, stirring continuously. Add the chocolate and Grand Marnier and turn off the heat as soon as the chocolate has melted. Leave the filling to cool.

Preheat the oven to 400°F/200°C/gas mark 6. Roll out the pastry to a thickness of ¼ inch/6 mm and use it to line the bottom and sides of a well-greased 10 inch/25 cm flan tin. Pour in the cool filling, trim the edge of the pastry, then bake the tart for 20 minutes. Unmould it on to an flameproof serving dish.

To make the meringue, cook 5 oz/150 g of the sugar with 2 tablespoons water to a temperature of 235°F/113°C, then briefly immerse the base of the pan in cold water to prevent further cooking. Beat the egg whites with a pinch of salt until very firm, then gradually pour in the hot sugar syrup, whisking continuously to obtain a shiny, firm meringue. Fold in the finely chopped almonds and 1 tablespoon of sugar. Pour the meringue over the tart and brown under the grill for 4 - 5 minutes. Serve immediately.

Orange Mousse with Chocolate

Mousse d'Arancia al Cioccolato

To serve 12

1¼ lb/600 g plain chocolate

12 fl oz/350 ml milk

4 egg yolks

4 oz/100 g sugar

1 oz/25 g flour

3 fl oz/75 ml Grand Marnier or other orange liqueur

grated rind of 3 oranges

½ pint/300 ml double cream

Preparation and cooking time: about 40 minutes, plus cooling

Break up the chocolate and melt it in a bain-marie until it reaches 113°F/45°C on a sugar thermometer. Immerse the bowl in cold water and, working the chocolate with a wooden spoon, cool to 86°-90°F/30°-31°C. Pour some of the chocolate into glass dishes to coat them. Spread out the remaining chocolate very thinly on a marble surface and leave it to cool.

Prepare the custard. Heat the milk. In a bowl, beat the egg yolks with the sugar and flour. Pour in the milk in a thin stream, then place over very low heat and, stirring continuously to avoid lumps, simmer for 3-4 minutes. Take off the heat and stir in the Grand Marnier and the orange rind. Leave to cool.

Whip the cream until very stiff and fold it into the cooled custard.

Using a knife with a wide, sharp blade, scrape the chocolate off the marble to make flakes. Divide the cold custard between the chocolate-lined dishes, decorate with the chocolate flakes and serve immediately, or keep in the refrigerator.

Bananas with Chocolate Sauce

Banane al Cioccolato

To serve 4

1 sheet of frozen puff pastry

butter for greasing the baking sheet

2 oz/50 g caster sugar, plus extra for dusting

5 oz/150 g plain chocolate

1 oz/25 g butter

4 small bananas, peeled and sliced

½ glass Cointreau

icing sugar

Preparation and cooking time: about 30 minutes, plus defrosting the pastry

Defrost the pastry. Preheat the oven to 400°F/200°C/gas mark 6. Roll out the defrosted pastry and cut into half-moon shapes. Arrange these on a greased baking sheet, sprinkle liberally with caster sugar and bake for about 10 minutes.

Meanwhile, chop the chocolate. Mix it with 4 fl oz/100 ml cold water in a bain-marie and melt, until it becomes a thick sauce, stirring.

Put the butter and remaining sugar in a frying pan and when the mixture becomes caramel coloured, brown the bananas over high heat. Moisten them with the Cointreau, tilt the pan towards the flame and flambé.

As soon as the alcohol has evaporated, arrange the bananas on 4 plates already prepared with a layer of chocolate sauce. Add the pastry half-moons and serve the bananas tepid, sprinkled with icing sugar.

Chocolate and Meringue Caskets (top left), **Chocolate Meringue Tart** *(bottom left)* **and** **Bananas with Chocolate Sauce** *(below)*

Panettone with Chocolate Mousse

Panettone con Mousse di Cioccolato

To serve 8-10

---

12 oz/350 g plain chocolate

---

2 fl oz/50 ml milk

---

6 fl oz/175 ml orange liqueur

---

2 eggs, separated plus 1 extra yolk

---

¹/₃ pint/200 ml whipping cream

---

1 x 2¹/₄ lb/1 kg panettone

Preparation and cooking time: about 40 minutes, plus freezing

To make the mousse, break up the chocolate and place it in a heatproof bowl. Add the milk and 2 fl oz/50 ml of the liqueur and melt in a bain-marie. Off the heat, add the 3 egg yolks. Beat the egg whites until very stiff. Whip the cream until very firm.

Up-turn the panettone on the work surface. Make an incision 1¹/₂ inches/ 4 cm from the edge and cut all round and three-quarters of the way down the cake (about 4 inches/10 cm from the bottom) to remove the inside. Using a long knife with a flexible blade, gradually cut into the vertical incision. Holding the knife handle firmly, rotate the blade so as to release the base of the soft inside and to remove it all in one piece.

Divide the inside of the panettone into 4 equal circles. Dilute the remaining liqueur with a little cold water and liberally brush the inside of the panettone and the circles with this mixture.

Keeping the panettone upside-down, fill with one-quarter of the mousse. Cover with a circle, then with another layer of mousse, and continue to make layers in this way, finishing with the circle from the base of the panettone. Turn it the right way up and freeze for at least 2 hours before serving.

Little Pastry Cases with Chocolate Mousse

Coupelle con Mousse al Cioccolato

To make 8-10

4 oz/100 g butter, plus extra for greasing the baking tray

4 egg whites, size 2

4 oz/100 g icing sugar

4 oz/100 g flour, plus extra for the baking tray

1 teaspoon vanilla essence

10 oz/300 g plain chocolate

2 fl oz/50 ml rum

9 fl oz/250 ml double cream

9 fl oz/250 ml milk

2 egg yolks

3 oz/75 g caster sugar

¹/₂ tablespoon flour

Preparation and cooking time: about 1 hour 40 minutes, plus chilling

First make the pastry cases. (You can do this the day before if you keep them in a cool, dry place.) Preheat the oven to 400°F/200°C/gas mark 6.

Melt the butter without browning it, then cool. In a bowl, mix together the unbeaten egg whites with the icing sugar, flour, half the vanilla and the cooled melted butter to make a soft paste.

Butter and flour a baking tray; on it place 1 tablespoon of the mixture, flattening it out with the back of a spoon to make a very thin disc 6-6¹/₂ inches/15-16 cm in diameter. Place the tray in the hot oven for about 4 minutes. Remove; the disc should be soft, pale in the centre and lightly browned at the edges. Lift it off the tray with a palette knife and mould it around the base of an up-turned cup. Leave to cool, then unmould. Repeat the procedure until all the paste is used up. (You should end up with 8 - 10 pastry cases.)

To make the mousse, break up the chocolate and place in a bowl with the rum. Stand the bowl in a pan with two fingers of tepid water, place over very low heat and melt the chocolate, stirring frequently and gently. Leave to cool. Whip the cream very stiffly. Fold it gently into the cooled chocolate. Refrigerate for about 2 hours.

Finally, prepare the sauce. Heat the milk and, meanwhile, mix the egg yolks with the sugar, remaining vanilla and flour. Stir in the hot milk. Pour the mixture back into the pan and heat over very low heat, stirring continuously; do not let it boil. Turn off the heat and leave the sauce to cool.

Just before serving, divide the mousse and vanilla sauce equally between the pastry cases.

Chocolate Roulade

Biscotto Arrotolato al Cioccolato

To serve 8

2 eggs, size 2, plus 2 extra yolks

3 oz/75 g caster sugar

3 oz/75 g flour

butter and flour for greasing

3 fl oz/75 ml Maraschino liqueur

7 oz/200 g plain chocolate

9 oz/250 g Mascarpone cheese

icing sugar and cocoa powder, for dusting

Preparation and cooking time: about 45 minutes, plus chilling

To make the sponge, preheat the oven to 375°F/190°C/gas mark 5. With an electric mixer, whisk the eggs with the sugar until light and fluffy. Sift in the flour from a height. Line a 16 x 13¹/₂ inch/ 40 x 34 cm baking tray with greaseproof paper and grease and flour the paper. Spoon in the sponge mixture, levelling the surface well with a small palette knife.

Bake the sponge in the preheated oven for about 15 minutes. Remove from the oven and invert on to a scrupulously clean tea cloth. Roll up in the cloth and leave to cool.

Dilute the Maraschino liqueur with 2 tablespoons cold water. Break up the chocolate and melt it in a bain-marie. When it has melted and is tepid, mix it with the 2 egg yolks and

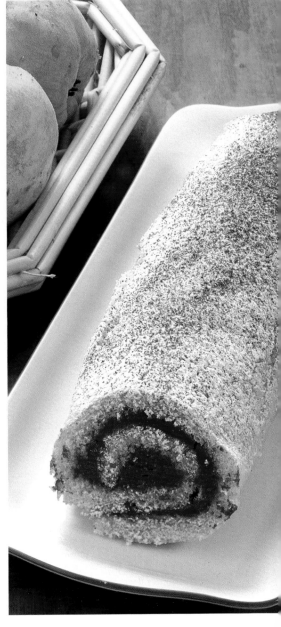

Mascarpone, working the mixture with a whisk to form a soft cream. Refrigerate for 20 minutes to firm up slightly.

Unroll the sponge. Moisten with the Maraschino mixture and spread with the cream. Roll up again, using the cloth to help you. Wrap the roulade in cling film and refrigerate for about 1 hour.

Just before serving, take the roulade out of the fridge, place on a serving plate and sift on a dusting of icing sugar and cocoa.

Panettone with Chocolate Mousse (left) and **Chocolate Roulade** (above)

Pistachio and Hazelnut Charlotte

Charlotte di Pistacchio e Nocciole

To serve 12

2 eggs, plus 3 extra yolks

5¹/₂ oz/165 g caster sugar, plus 1 tablespoon

¹/₂ teaspoon vanilla essence

3 oz/75 g flour, plus extra for the tin

grated rind of ¹/₂ lemon

4 oz/100 g hazelnuts, toasted and skinned

2 oz/50 g plain chocolate

9 fl oz/250 ml double cream

3 tablespoons powdered gelatine

9 fl oz/250 ml milk

2 teaspoons cornflour

4 oz/100 g pistachios, blanched and skinned

Preparation and cooking time: about 1³/₄ hours plus 6 hours' chilling

Preheat the oven to 425°F/220°C/gas mark 7. Beat the whole eggs, 3 oz/75 g sugar and vanilla together until light and fluffy. Sift the flour with the grated lemon rind and fold delicately into the egg mixture.

Butter and flour a 9 inch/23 cm long Swiss roll tin and line with greaseproof paper. Butter and flour the paper, pour in the sponge mixture and level the surface. Bake for about 10 minutes. Turn out the sponge on to a tea towel and set aside.

Grind the hazelnuts finely with 1 tablespoon sugar in a food processor to make a paste. Break the chocolate into pieces and place in a bowl with 2 fl oz/50 ml of the unwhipped cream and the hazelnut paste. Set the bowl in a pan with two fingers of water and melt the chocolate over very low heat.

Soften the gelatine in cold water. Heat the milk. Beat the 3 egg yolks with the remaining sugar and the cornflour. Add the hot milk, stir in the gelatine, then set over very low heat and heat, stirring continuously; do not let it boil.

Divide the cream into 4 equal parts. Add the chocolate mixture to one-quarter of the cream and pistachios to another quarter. Blend the latter until smooth. Whip all the remaining cream and fold in two-thirds of this into the pistachio cream. Chill in the fridge for about 20 minutes.

To assemble the charlotte, line a loose-based round cake tin, 10 inches/25 cm diameter, 3¹/₂ inches/9 cm deep, with some of the sponge base. Fold the remaining whipped cream into the chocolate cream. Take the pistachio cream out of the refrigerator (it should have begun to set) and pour it into the tin. Spread the chocolate cream on top. Cover with slices of sponge. Chill in the refrigerator for about 6 hours. Unmould and serve.

Chocolate and Pistachio Baskets

Coupelle al Cioccolata e Pistacchio

To make 12

3 oz/75 g flour

2 eggs, separated

2 oz/50 g icing sugar

2 oz/50 g butter, melted and cooled

9 fl oz/ 250 ml milk

3 oz/75 g caster sugar

¹/₂ teaspoon vanilla essence

2 oz/50 g pistachios, shelled, peeled and finely chipped, plus a few whole pistachios for decoration

2 oz/50 g blanched almonds, finely chopped

4 oz/100 g plain chocolate

Break up the chocolate and place in a bowl with the chopped hazelnuts and unwhipped cream. Stand the bowl in a bain-marie and set over moderate heat until the chocolate melts, then add the Amaretto liqueur.

Remove the bowl from the bain-marie and leave the mixture to cool, then whisk it until dense but still malleable. (Place the mixture in the fridge from time to time during this procedure.)

When the mixture is dense, chill in the fridge for 30 minutes, then, with the aid of a spoon, divide it into 25 equal pieces. Roll each piece liberally in cocoa powder to make small balls (truffles). Place in paper cases and decorate each truffle with a hazelnut. Keep in the fridge until ready to serve.

Pistachio and Hazelnut Charlotte (opposite), **Chocolate and Pistachio Baskets** *(left) and* **Hazelnut Truffles** *(below)*

Preparation and cooking time: about 1 hour 20 minutes

First prepare the baskets. (This can be done the day before; keep them in a cool dry place). Preheat the oven to 400°F/200°C/gas mark 6. In a bowl beat 2 oz/50 g of the flour with the egg whites, icing sugar and cooled melted butter. Line a baking sheet with a sheet of baking parchment, put on 1 tablespoon of the mixture and flatten it with the back of the spoon to make a thin 3¹/₂ inches/9 cm round. Add 2 more rounds. Bake in the preheated oven for 3-4 minutes, until lightly browned at the edges and pale in the centre. Remove from the oven and, while still warm, mould one inside a coffee cup. The dough will harden as it cools and can be formed into a basket. Make 12 baskets this way.

To make the pastry cream, heat the milk without letting it boil. Mix the egg yolks with the caster sugar and remaining flour, then pour on the hot milk in a steady stream. Return the mixture to the milk pan, set over a moderate heat and simmer for 4-5 minutes, stirring continuously to prevent lumps from forming. Take off the heat and stir in the vanilla. Leave to cool, then add the chopped pistachios and almonds.

Just before serving, coarsely chop the chocolate and melt it in a bain-marie. Brush it lavishly over the insides of the baskets. Leave to harden, then place the pistachio filling in a piping bag with a plain nozzle and fill up the baskets. Garnish with whole pistachios and serve.

Hazelnut Truffles

Tartufi alla Nocciola

To make 25

7 oz/200 g plain chocolate

2 oz/50 g hazelnuts, shelled, toasted and finely chopped, plus 25 whole nuts for decoration

4 fl oz/100 ml whipping cream

1¹/₂ fl oz/40 ml Amaretto liqueur

cocoa powder

Preparation time: about 1 hour, plus chilling

Chestnut and Chocolate Roll

'Salame' di Castagne e Cioccolato

To serve 12

5 oz/150 g butter, softened

4 oz/100 g icing sugar

3 oz/75 g cocoa powder

4 tablespoons Amaretto liqueur

6-7 macaroons

12 oz/350 g chestnuts, boiled and puréed

chocolate vermicelli

a little whipping cream

Preparation and cooking time: about 40 minutes, plus 3-4 hours' chilling

Beat the butter in a bowl with a wooden spoon until light and frothy. Sift in the icing sugar and the cocoa and mix in half the Amaretto. Grind the macaroons almost to a powder and add them, together with the chestnut paste and the remaining liqueur, reserving 1 teaspoon. Blend all the ingredients together smoothly.

Pour the reserved teaspoon of Amaretto, diluted with 2 tablespoons of cold water, on to a sheet of foil. Spread the chestnut mixture on the foil and roll it up evenly and tightly. Seal the ends and refrigerate for 3-4 hours.

Just before serving, take the roll out of the refrigerator and remove the foil. Slice with a very sharp knife dipped in a bowl of hot water. Decorate, if you like, with a stripe of chocolate vermicelli and serve with whipped cream.

Rich Chocolate Cake

Torta 'Gianfranco'

To serve 10

a little butter and flour for the tin

3 eggs, plus 2 egg yolks

8 oz/225 g caster sugar

a pinch of salt

1 sachet of vanilla sugar

10 oz/300 g plain chocolate

4 oz/100 g flour

2 oz/50 g potato flour

3 tablespoons cocoa powder

1 heaped teaspoon baking powder

¹/₄ pint/150 ml milk

14 fl oz/400 ml whipping cream

2 oz/50 g flaked almonds

Preparation and cooking time: about 1³/₄ hours, plus 4-5 hours' chilling

Butter a 10 inch/25 cm round cake tin and sprinkle with flour. Whisk the whole eggs briskly with 5 oz/150 g of the sugar, salt and the vanilla sugar until they form soft peaks.

Preheat the oven to 350°F/180°C/gas mark 4. Melt 3 oz/75 g of the chocolate over low heat and leave to cool. Mix all but 1 tablespoon of the flour with the potato flour, cocoa and the baking powder and sift into the egg mixture, carefully folding in with a wooden spoon. Fold in the melted chocolate and pour the mixture into the prepared pan. Bake in the oven for about 30 minutes.

Meanwhile, beat the egg yolks with the remaining 1 tablespoon of flour, sugar and a pinch of salt. Gradually add the milk and bring to the boil, stirring constantly. Remove the pan from the heat and leave to cool, stirring from time to time.

Cut 4 oz/100 g of the chocolate into small pieces, then melt it over low heat and add it to the mixture, stirring vigorously. Leave to cool.

Turn the cake out on to a wire rack. Whip the cream until stiff, then fold it into the chocolate mixture. Cut the cake into 3 layers and sandwich together with two-thirds of the chocolate mixture. Coat top and sides of cake with some of the chocolate mixture and sprinkle with the remainder of the chocolate, grated. Pipe rosettes of chocolate mixture on the cake and decorate with flaked almonds. Refrigerate and serve within 4-5 hours.

Little Chocolate Puddings

Budinetti al Cioccolato

To make 8

5 oz/150 g plain chocolate

14 fl oz/400 ml milk

¹/₃ pint/200 ml whipping cream

4 eggs, plus 4 extra yolks

10 oz/300 g caster sugar, plus 2 tablespoons

2 oranges

1¹/₂ fl oz/40 ml double cream

Preparation and cooking time: about 1 hour, plus at least 6 hours' chilling

Preheat the oven to 375°F/190°C/gas mark 5. Break the chocolate into pieces and heat it with the milk and cream until melted.

In a bowl, whisk the eggs and yolks lightly with 5 oz/150 g of sugar. Gradually pour the milk mixture on to the eggs, mixing well.

Divide the mixture between 8 crème caramel moulds or ramekins, stand in a bain-marie filled with hot, but not boiling, water and cook in the oven for about 50 minutes. Leave to cool, then place in the fridge and chill for at least another 6 hours.

Pare off the orange rinds and squeeze the oranges. Measure the juice; you should have ¼ pint/150 ml; squeeze another orange if necessary. In a small saucepan, bring the juice to the boil with 2 tablespoons sugar and ¼ pint/150 ml water. Add a few strands of orange rind and boil until you obtain a light syrup. Stir in the cream and leave to cool.

In another saucepan, boil the remaining rind with the remaining 5 oz/150 g sugar and a very little water. Boil until the water has evaporated and the sugar has caramelized the rind.

Unmould the chocolate puddings on to serving plates, pour over the cold orange syrup and top with a little heap of rind. Serve immediately.

knife and use it to halve the chocolate egg lengthways, to give 2 empty shells.

Sprinkle the sponge fingers with the Maraschino liqueur, then dip them into the caramel to coat them. Whip the cream until very stiff. Break up the sponge fingers and put 3 in each egg shell, alternating them with about half the cream.

Put the remaining cream in a piping bag with a fluted nozzle and fill the shells with rosettes of cream. Decorate with a little grated chocolate and refrigerate until ready to serve.

Chestnut and Chocolate Roll (opposite), **Little Chocolate Puddings** *(above) and* **Caramel-filled Easter Egg** *(below)*

Caramel-filled Easter Egg

Uovo Pasquale al Caramello

To serve 4

5 oz/150 g caster sugar

1 x 5 oz/150 g hollow chocolate egg

6 sponge fingers

Maraschino liqueur

14 fl oz/400 ml whipping cream

grated chocolate for decoration

Preparation time: about 30 minutes

Put the sugar in a saucepan with 4 tablespoons cold water, set over moderate heat and cook to a golden caramel.

Meanwhile, heat a long-bladed

Zabaglione Dessert

Chiaroscuro allo Zabaione

To serve 4-6

3 eggs

2 oz/50 g sugar

8 tablespoons dry Marsala wine

1 oz/25 g sultanas

1/3 pint/200 ml whipping cream

12 chocolate-covered Savoy biscuits

Preparation and cooking time:
about 30 minutes

Separate the eggs, placing the yolks in a saucepan with the sugar. Stir with a wooden spoon until pale and frothy, then stir in 6 tablespoons of the Marsala wine, one at a time. Heat the mixture in a double boiler, beating constantly with a small whisk until it thickens. Leave to cool.

Meanwhile, soak the sultanas for 15 minutes in warm water. When the zabaglione is cold, whip the cream and carefully stir in 3 tablespoons of it. Refrigerate the rest of the cream until it is required for decoration. Drain the sultanas thoroughly and stir in these, too. Then spoon the mixture into a deep, square dish, distributing it evenly.

Pour 2 tablespoons of the Marsala wine into a soup bowl and add 2 tablespoons of water. Briefly dip the Savoy biscuits in the mixture, keeping the chocolate-coated sides uppermost as you dip. Arrange the biscuits diagonally on top of the zabaglione as you proceed, alternating the chocolate sides with the plain. Cut the biscuits to fit the dish without leaving any gaps.

Put the remaining whipped cream into a piping bag with a fluted round nozzle and make a decorative border of swirls around the Savoy biscuits. Refrigerate until serving time.

Zabaglione Dessert (top), **Chocolate and Amaretti Cream Cups** *(right) and* **Caramelized Chocolate Cushion** *(far right)*

Chocolate and Amaretti Cream Cups

Crema in Tazza al Cioccolato e Amaretti

To serve 8

¹⁄₃ oz/6 g leaf gelatine

5 egg yolks

7 oz/200 g icing sugar

18 fl oz/500 ml milk

7 oz/200 g plain chocolate, chopped

4 oz/100 g Amaretti biscuits

4 fl oz/100 ml whipping cream, whipped

glacé cherries

wafer curls, to decorate

Preparation and cooking time: about 30 minutes, plus chilling

Soak the gelatine in cold water. In a bowl, whisk the egg yolks with the icing sugar, then gradually pour in the cold milk. Pour the mixture into a saucepan and add the chopped chocolate. Heat the custard over a very moderate heat just until the chocolate melts; do not let it boil.

Crush the Amaretti biscuits in a food processor, and thoroughly squeeze out the gelatine. Add both to the custard. Take the pan off the heat and stir the custard for another couple of seconds, then divide it between 8 cups and leave to cool before refrigerating for at least 2 hours.

Just before serving, decorate each cup with a rosette of whipped cream, a glacé cherry and a couple of wafer curls.

Caramelized Chocolate Cushion

Mattonella al Cioccolato Caramellata

To serves 8

6 eggs, size 3, plus 3 extra yolks

14 oz/400 g caster sugar

a pinch of salt

½ teaspoon vanilla essence

4 oz/100 g flour

butter and flour for the cake tin

5 oz/150 g plain chocolate

5 oz/150 g mixed glacé fruit, plus extra glacé cherries for decoration

½ pint/300 ml milk

14 fl oz/400 ml whipping cream

cocoa powder for dusting

Preparation and cooking time: about 4 hours, plus 2½ hours' chilling

First make a sponge cake. (This can be done several days in advance; wrap in cling film and keep in a cool place until needed.) Preheat the oven to 350°F/180°C/gas mark 4. With an electric mixer, whisk 3 whole eggs and 4 oz/100 g of the sugar with the salt to a ribbon consistency. Stir in the vanilla, then sift in the flour from a height, folding it in with a wooden spoon from bottom to top and vice versa. Grease and flour an 8½ inch/22 cm cake pan and spoon in the sponge mixture. Bake in the preheated oven for about 35 minutes.

To check the baking, insert a skewer into the centre; if it comes out dry, the sponge is ready. Remove from the oven, unmould on to a wire rack and leave to cool.

Just before assembling the pillow, pour 5 oz/150 g of the remaining sugar into a flameproof rectangular loaf tin. Place on the heat until the sugar dissolves and caramelizes the base and sides of the tin. Take off the heat and leave the caramel to cool.

Meanwhile, preheat the oven to 190°C/375°F/gas mark 5. Slice the sponge cake, scrape the chocolate into slivers and finely dice the fruit. Whisk the remaining eggs, 3 yolks and remaining sugar together, then add the milk.

Make alternating layers of sponge, chocolate and fruit in the caramelized mould. Pour over the egg mixture, making sure that it fills the spaces between the layers. Place the mould in another tin filled with two fingers of water and bake the dessert in this bain-marie for 2½ hours in the preheated oven. Remove from the oven and leave to cool.

Just before serving, whip the cream and put it in a piping bag with a star nozzle. Unmould the dessert on to a serving plate and decorate with whirls of cream, glacé cherries and a dusting of cocoa.

Chocolate Bavarois

Bavarese al Cioccolato

To serve 10

$^1/_2$ oz/12 g leaf gelatine

9 fl oz/250 ml milk

3 egg yolks

4 oz/100 g caster sugar

1 pint/600 ml whipping cream

5 oz/150 g mixed glacé fruits

Kirsch

7 oz/200 g plain chocolate

$^3/_4$ oz/20 g icing sugar

11 sponge fingers

Preparation time: 1 hour, plus 12 hours' chilling

Soak the gelatine and bring the milk to the boil. Meanwhile, put the egg yolks and sugar in a saucepan and mix together, then gradually pour on the hot milk, stirring very carefully. Immediately place the pan on the heat, add the well-softened and squeezed gelatine and dissolve it in the custard, mixing continuously. When steam begins to rise from the custard, take the pan off the heat and leave to cool. (To speed up the process, immerse the pan in cold water.) Refrigerate the cool custard.

Meanwhile, whip $^1/_2$ pint/300 ml of the cream very stiffly and finely chop the glacé fruits, then steep them in Kirsch. As soon as the custard in the fridge begins to set (it should be gelatinous but not too firm, or it will be difficult to mix), remove it from the fridge and stir in the fruit then the Kirsch, then the whipped cream, folding it in extremely lightly. Transfer the mixture into a bavarois mould dampened with cold water and drained, level the surface well and

chill in the fridge for at least 12 hours.

Decorate the bavarois shortly before serving. Grate and melt 5 oz/150 g of the chocolate in a bowl set in a bain-marie of boiling water, stirring occasionally with a scrupulously clean wooden spoon. Spread out the sponge fingers on a tray. When the chocolate is melted and smooth, spoon it over the sponge fingers, coating the top surfaces. Whip the remaining cream very stiffly and delicately fold in the icing sugar.

Unmould the bavarois on to a round serving plate and arrange the sponge fingers around the sides, spacing them evenly, with the chocolate side outwards.

Put the whipped cream in a piping bag with a fluted nozzle and decorate the bavarois with stripes of cream between the sponge fingers and rosettes on the top of the ends of the biscuits. Grate the remaining chocolate, sprinkle it over the centre of the bavarois, and serve.

Chocolate-glazed Biscuits

Biscottini Glassati al Cioccolato

To serve 6

6 oz/175 g butter, diced

9 oz/250 g flour

2 oz/50 g desiccated coconut

4 oz/100 g caster sugar

2 oz/50 g blanched almonds, finely chopped with 2 oz/50 g shelled hazelnuts

centre and add the coconut, sugar, chopped almonds and hazelnuts, the egg, salt and the cinnamon. Knead to a dough, then roll into a long sausage shape and cut into slices. Flatten these into thin wafers. Arrange on a baking sheet lined with greaseproof paper and bake in the hot oven for 13 minutes. Remove the biscuits from the oven and leave to cool.

Break up the chocolate and melt it in a bain-marie, then brush it liberally over one side of the biscuits. Place them, chocolate sides up, on a sheet of kitchen paper to set. As soon as the chocolate has dried completely, sprinkle the biscuits with icing sugar.

---

1 egg

---

a large pinch of salt

---

a small pinch of ground cinnamon

---

5 oz/150 g plain chocolate

---

icing sugar

Preparation and cooking time: about 1 hour

Preheat the oven to 400°F/200°C/gas mark 6. Using your fingertips, rub the butter with the flour until they resemble a mound of breadcrumbs. Place on the work surface, make a well in the

Coronets of Choux Buns

Coroncine di Bignè

To serve 8

---

7 oz/200 g flour

---

5 oz/150 g butter, plus extra for greasing

---

salt

---

5 eggs

4¹/₂ oz /130 g plain chocolate

---

2 fl oz/50 ml Crème de Cacao liqueur

---

14 fl oz/400 ml whipping cream, plus a little extra for decoration

---

5 oz/150 g caster sugar, plus 4-5 tablespoons extra for the sauce

---

9 oz/250 g ready-to-eat dried apricots

---

2 oz/50 g raspberries

Grand Marnier

Preparation and cooking time: about 2 hours

Make the choux buns following the instructions on page 16 for Profiteroles in Spun Caramel, using the flour, 4 oz/100 g of the butter, a pinch of salt and the 5 whole eggs, beating them in one at a time. You should obtain about 40 buns. You can make these a day in advance if it is more convenient.

Shortly before serving, prepare the filling. Break up the chocolate and melt it in a bain-marie with the Crème de Cacao. Meanwhile, whip the cream and stir it into the melted chocolate, stirring continuously. Refrigerate the mixture for 20 minutes.

Make an incision in the base of each choux bun and fill them with the chocolate mixture. Arrange 5 buns in a coronet on 8 serving plates.

Make a caramel with 5 oz/150 g sugar and one-third of a glass of water, then pour the caramel over the buns.

Slowly heat 4 - 5 tablespoons sugar with the remaining butter to obtain a caramel. Add the halved apricots and the whole raspberries and turn them in the caramel. Moisten with Grand Marnier and flambé. As soon as the alcohol has evaporated, pour the sauce into the centre of the coronets and around the edge, and decorate with a dollop of whipped cream. Serve immediately, before the choux buns become soggy.

Chocolate Bavarois (far left),
Cholocate-glazed Biscuits (above)
and Coronets of Choux Buns (left)

Coconut and Chocolate Bavarois

Bavarese di Cocco e Cioccolato

To serve 8-10

1 coconut

1¼ pint/750 ml whipping cream

8 oz/225 g caster sugar

18 fl oz/500 ml milk

20 g/¾ oz leaf gelatine

Kirsch

3 egg yolks

1 teaspoon cornflour

1½ oz/40 g plain chocolate

16 strands of fresh coconut

10 strands of candied citrus peel

12 chocolate wafer cigarettes

Preparation time: about 1 hour, plus 8 hours' setting and 12 hours' infusing

1) Break open the coconut, discard the water, then peel with a vegetable peeler to obtain about 10 oz/300 g flesh. Purée this in food processor.

2) Place the puréed coconut in a saucepan with ½ pint/300 ml of the cream, 5 oz/150 g of the sugar and 9 fl oz/250 ml of the milk, and leave to infuse for 12 hours. Soak just over half the gelatine in a bowl of cold water.

3) Place the saucepan containing the coconut mixture over moderate heat and heat without boiling, then squeeze out the gelatine, add it to the coconut mixture and stir to dissolve. Take the pan off the heat and leave to cool.

4) Press the coconut mixture through a fine sieve lined with muslin. Pour the resulting mixture into a 4½ pint/ 2.5 litre mould brushed with Kirsch, then refrigerate.

5) Beat the egg yolks with 3 oz/75 g of the sugar and the cornflour, and gradually pour in the remaining milk, which should be heated. Pour the mixture into a saucepan, add the chocolate and the remaining soaked and squeezed gelatine.

6) When the mixture begins to thicken, whip the remaining cream and stir in. Pour this mixture over the set coconut bavarois in the mould. Refrigerate for at least 8 hours before serving.

1

2

3

4

5

6

CAKES

The Italians are masters when it comes to making fabulous cakes — both scrumptious to eat and ravishingly beautiful to look at. Cakes lend style and elegance to any table — so much so that it sometimes seems a shame to destroy such wonderful creations by eating them. Force yourself, though. Don't hold back — it willl be worth every moment for that wonderful explosion of flavours!

Zabaione Charlotte

Charlotte allo Zabaione

To serve 8

6 egg yolks

4 oz/100 g caster sugar

9 fl oz/250 ml Marsala wine

2 fl oz/50 ml sweet white wine

14 fl oz/400 ml whipping cream

4 small cups of strong coffee

42 sponge fingers

cocoa powder

Preparation time: about 40 minutes, plus chilling

Put the egg yolks in a saucepan and add the sugar, Marsala and wine. Place over very low heat and whisk continuously until the mixture thickens into a very creamy, foamy zabaione, taking care not to let it boil. Take the pan off the heat, transfer the zabaione to a bowl and leave to cool.

Meanwhile, whip the cream until stiff. When the zabaione is cool, delicately fold in half the whipped cream. Dilute the coffee with a glass of water. Spread out 30 sponge fingers in a dish and pour over the coffee. Line the base of a 7¹/₂ inch/ 19 cm,5 inch/12 cm deep charlotte mould with greaseproof paper and lay on a layer of coffee-soaked sponge fingers. Cover with about one-third of the zabaione. Make a second layer of sponge fingers and continue to make layers in this way, finishing with sponge fingers. Place the mould in the freezer for at least 1 hour.

Unmould the charlotte on to a serving plate, remove the paper and sprinkle the dessert with sifted cocoa powder. Spread a little of the remaining whipped cream over the sides and stick on the 12 unsoaked sponge fingers, spacing them apart. Put the remaining cream into a piping bag with a fluted nozzle and decorate the charlotte with a grid of whipped cream on top, and stripes between the sponge fingers. Serve immediately, or keep the charlotte refrigerated until ready to serve.

Pink Cushion

Mattonella Rosa

To serve 8

4 eggs, plus 4 extra yolks

10 oz/300 g caster sugar

1 teaspoon vanilla essence

a pinch of salt

7 oz/200 g flour

butter and flour for the tin and greaseproof paper

¹/₂ pint/300 ml milk

Alchermes or Maraschino liqueur

12 oz/350 g shop-bought fondant icing

¹/₄ pint/150 ml whipping cream, whipped

Preparation and cooking time: about 12 hours

To make a sponge, preheat the oven to 400°F/200°C/gas mark 6. Whisk the 4 whole eggs with 5 oz/150 g of the sugar and ¹/₂ teaspoon of the vanilla, using a hand-held or electric mixer, until pale and of a ribbon consistency. Sift the salt mixed with the flour lightly over the mixture, then fold it in delicately. Grease a 16 x 13¹/₂ inch/40 x 34 cm Swiss roll tin and line it with greaseproof paper. Lightly grease and flour the paper, then spread on the sponge mixture into a regular rectangle. Bake in the preheated oven for about 15 minutes. Remove the baked sponge from the oven, invert it on to a clean tea towel and leave to cool.

Meanwhile, prepare the pastry cream. Heat the milk and flavour it with ¹/₂ teaspoon vanilla. Whisk the egg yolks with the remaining 5 oz/150 g sugar and remaining 2 oz/50 g flour in a small saucepan, then gradually pour in the hot milk. Place on low heat and cook the pastry cream for about 10 minutes until thickened, stirring continuously with a wooden spoon.

Cut the cooled sponge into 3 equal rectangles. Brush one with a little liqueur, then cover with about half the pastry cream. Top with the second sponge rectangle and repeat the procedure, reserving a few spoonfuls of pastry cream to decorate the finished dessert. Finish with the third sponge rectangle and brush this with liqueur. Spread the reserved pastry cream over the sides of the dessert.

In a bain-marie, melt the fondant icing to the consistency of thick cream (if necessary, dilute it with a few drops of water) and colour it with a dash of liqueur. Pour over the top of the dessert and spread evenly with a palette knife. Place the whipped cream in a piping bag with a fluted nozzle and decorate the sides of the dessert by piping on lines of whipped cream.

Luscious Cherry Cake

Dolce Cremoso alle Ciliegie

To serve 8

8 oz/225 g fresh cherries

8 oz/225 g sugar

1 stick cinnamon

1 clove

6 tablespoons dry white wine

³/₄ oz/20 g powdered gelatine

2 eggs, plus 2 extra yolks

grated rind of ¹/₂ lemon

a pinch of salt

1¹/₂ oz/40 g flour

1 pint/600 ml milk

8 oz/225 g sponge cake, thinly sliced

6 tablespoons Cointreau

Preparation and cooking time: about 1 hour, plus chilling

Stem the cherries, wash them and drain them well. Remove the stones and place the cherries in a small saucepan. Add 2 oz/50 g of the sugar, a small piece of cinnamon, the clove and the white wine. Cook the cherries over a moderate heat for about 15 minutes, until they are tender and the liquid has a syrupy consistency; allow to cool.

Meanwhile, dissolve the gelatine in cold water. In a small saucepan, beat the eggs and egg yolks together with the remaining sugar, the lemon rind, salt and the sifted flour. When creamy and smooth, dilute the mixture with the cold milk, poured in a trickle. Place over the heat and, stirring constantly, bring the mixture to the boil. Remove from the heat and add the gelatine, mixing to make sure it dissolves.

Line a rectangular cake pan measuring 10 x 5 inches/25 x 12 cm with foil. Pour some of the hot custard into it, then arrange some thin slices of sponge cake on top. Sprinkle lightly with Cointreau. Spread over the sponge cake a few cooked cherries drained of syrup (the syrup will be used at the end to moisten the cake), cover with some more of the custard, sponge cake and cherries. Continue with the layers until you have used up all the ingredients.

Leave the cake to cool, then place in the refrigerator for at least 2 hours or in the freezer for about 30 minutes or until the cake is quite firm. Then turn out on to a serving plate, pour the cherry syrup over it and serve.

Zabaione Charlotte (top left) and *Pink Cushion* (bottom left)

Strawberry and Cointreau Cake

Cuore di Mamma

To serve 8-10

2 eggs, plus 3 extra yolks

5 oz/150 g sugar

a little vanilla sugar

a pinch of salt

3 oz/75 g flour

2 oz/ 50 g potato flour

a little butter for greasing cake tin

1 tablespoon powdered gelatine

6 tablespoons dry Marsala wine

1 tablespoon brandy

⅓ pint/200 ml whipping cream

Strawberry and Cointreau Cake

5 oz/150 g fresh strawberries

6 tablespoons Cointreau

Preparation and cooking time: about 2 hours, plus at least 2 hours' chilling

Preheat the oven to 350°F/180°C/gas mark 4. Beat 2 whole eggs with 4 oz/100 g of the sugar, a little vanilla sugar and the salt until light and fluffy. Sift and fold in all but 2 tablespoons of the flour and the potato flour.

Butter a 3 pint/1.8 litre heart-shaped cake tin, sprinkle in the remaining flour and pour in the mixture. Bake for about 20 minutes or until a wooden skewer pushed into the centre of the cake comes out clean. Turn out on to a wire rack and leave to cool. Clean the cake tin.

Soak the gelatine in cold water. Beat the 3 egg yolks with the remaining sugar until white and fluffy. Blend in the Marsala wine and then the brandy. Heat the mixture and

bring it almost to the boil, stirring constantly. Pour the mixture into a bowl and blend in the gelatine immediately. Leave to cool, stirring from time to time. Finally, whip the cream and fold it into the mixture.

Hull and wash the strawberries and slice them finely. Line the bottom of the cleaned cake tin with greaseproof paper and brush it with a little Cointreau. Return the heart-shaped cake to the tin and make holes in it with a fork. Sprinkle with the remaining Cointreau.

Pour half the prepared gelatine mixture on to the cake and sprinkle it with half the strawberries. Cover with the rest of the mixture and sprinkle with the remaining strawberries. Tap the cake tin gently and place it in the refrigerator for a least 2 hours.

Once the filling has set, run a knife around the edge of the cake and invert it on to a plate. Keep in the refrigerator until ready to serve.

Chocolate Cream Gâteau

Pagoda di Castagne

To serve 8

8 oz/225 g chestnut purée

7oz/200 g Mascarpone cheese or cream cheese

4 oz/100 g icing sugar

1 oz/25 g cocoa powder

2 tablespoons brandy

3 tablespoons Amaretto liqueur

1/4 pint/150 ml whipping cream

1 sponge cake, about 9 in/23 cm

4 fl oz/100 ml Cointreau

1 tablespoon chocolate vermicelli

1 tablespoon white chocolate chips

6 chocolate buttons

Preparation time: about 1 1/2 hours

Place the chestnut purée in a bowl and beat in the Mascarpone cheese, stirring with a wooden spoon until smooth. Sift over 3 oz/75 g of icing sugar and the cocoa powder, and mix well, then add the brandy and

Amaretto liqueur, making sure that each tablespoon is thoroughly absorbed before adding the next.

Whip the cream until stiff, then fold in the rest of the sifted icing sugar, stirring with a wooden spoon from top to bottom rather than round and round. Spoon the cream into a piping bag with a small round nozzle, and keep in the refrigerator.

Place the sponge cake on a serving dish and moisten it with the Cointreau, then sieve on to it the mixture of chestnuts and Mascarpone cheese, arranging it in a small heap. Pipe the sweetened whipped cream around the edge, and sprinkle over the chocolate vermicelli. Complete the decoration of the cake by placing the white chocolate chips on top of it and arranging the chocolate buttons evenly spread around it.

Keep the cake in the least cold part of the refrigerator until serving time. If you wish, instead of using sponge cake as a base, you can use any other kind of risen cake such as panettone, Viennese pastry or so on.

Coffee Cream Puff

Sfogliata alla Crema di Caffè

To serve 10

1 lb/450 g puff pastry

4 oz/100 g butter

8 almonds

1 egg

4 oz/100 g Mascarpone cheese

4 oz/100 g icing sugar

2 tablespoons freeze-dried instant coffee

2 tablespoons coffee liqueur

2 tablespoons brandy

12 Savoy biscuits

1/4 pint/150 ml Amaretto liqueur

Preparation and cooking time: about 1 hour, plus any defrosting

Defrost the pastry if necessary. Preheat the oven to 375°F/190°C/gas mark 5. Cut the butter into small pieces and leave to soften.

Meanwhile, finely chop the almonds. Divide the pastry in half and roll it out into two rounds, each 10 inches/25 cm in diameter. Place on 2 baking trays and prick with a fork all over. Separate the egg yolk from the white and brush the surface of the pastry with the white. Bake for about 20 minutes, or until the pastry is golden brown. Remove from the oven and place on a cooling rack.

Meanwhile, beat the butter with the Mascarpone cheese and the icing sugar, ideally with an electric mixer. Incorporate the egg yolk, the instant coffee, the coffee liqueur and the brandy. The cream should be light and fluffy by the time you have finished.

Lay one pastry round on top of the other and trim until they are exactly the same size. (Keep the offcuts.) Place one round on a round cardboard cake base and spread one third of the coffee cream over it. Soak the Savoy biscuits in the Amaretto and arrange these on top of the cream, breaking them up so that they do not jut out. Spread half the remaining cream over the biscuits. Then sprinkle over the crumbled pastry offcuts and press down the second pastry round to ensure it adheres to the cream.

Cover the cake with the remaining cream and decorate with the chopped almonds. Place on a cake stand and refrigerate for at least 30 minutes before serving. Finally, sprinkle with a little icing sugar or decorate as you please.

Orange Tart with Whipped Cream

Crostata all'Arancia con Panna Montata

To serve 6-8

4 oz/100 g butter

12 oz/350 g flour

1 egg, plus 4 extra yolks

4 oz/100 g icing sugar

1 teaspoon ground cinnamon

5 oz/150 g caster sugar

5 oranges

18 fl oz/500 ml milk

2 tablespoons orange liqueur

flour and butter for the work surface and tin

1/3 pint/200ml whipping cream

4 oz/100 g apricot jam

Preparation and cooking time: about 1 1/2 hours

First make the pastry. Mix together the butter with 10 oz/300 g of the flour, then place on the work surface and make a well in the centre. Break the egg into the centre and add the icing sugar and the cinnamon. Knead fairly quickly to prevent the butter softening too much, then wrap the pastry in cling film and refrigerate for about 30 minutes.

Meanwhile, make the filling. In a bowl, beat the 4 egg yolks with the caster sugar, remaining flour and the grated rind of one orange. Heat the milk and gradually pour it on to the egg mixture, then pour it back into the milk pan and place over low heat. Simmer the custard for 5 minutes, stirring continuously to avoid lumps, then add the liqueur and leave to cool.

Preheat the oven to 375°F/190°C/ gas mark 5. On a lightly floured surface, roll out the pastry into a 3/8 inch/4mm thick circle. Use it to line a greased and floured 10 1/2 inch/ 26 cm springform tin. Fill with the cold custard. Trim off the excess pastry from the edges and crimp the border. Bake the base in the hot oven for about 40 minutes.

Meanwhile, prepare the decoration. Peel 3 oranges, paring off all the white membrane, and cut into slices. Whip the cream very stiffly. Dilute the jam with one-third of a glass of water and boil for 3 minutes. Pare off the rind from the remaining orange and cut into very thin slivers. Blanch in boiling water for 2 minutes and drain thoroughly.

Remove the tart base from the oven, unmould it on to a serving plate and leave to cool. Arrange the sliced oranges on the filling and glaze with the tepid apricot jam. Fill a piping bag with a fluted nozzle with the whipped cream and pipe a border of cream rosettes around the tart. Finish with a sprinkling of orange rind.

Semifreddo Ice Cream with Raspberry Sauce

Semifreddo con Salsa ai Lamponi

To serve 8

5 eggs, 3 separated, plus 1 extra yolk

17 oz/475 g caster sugar

a pinch of salt

3/4 teaspoon vanilla essence

5 oz/150 g flour

butter and flour for the tin

18 fl oz/500 ml milk

grated rind of 1 lemon

1 pint/600 ml whipping cream

Maraschino liqueur

4 oz/100 g fresh raspberries

coloured sugar shapes

Preparation time: about 2 hours, plus freezing

To make the sponge base, preheat the oven to 350°F/180°C/gas mark 4. Whisk 2 eggs and 3 oz/75 g of the sugar together with the salt and 1/4 teaspoon vanilla by hand or with an electric mixer until any mixture that falls off the whisk remains on the surface and does not immediately sink back into the mixture in the bowl. Sift in 3 oz/75 g of the flour from a height, folding it in delicately, working from bottom to top and vice versa. Grease a 16 x 13¹/₂ inch/40 x 34 cm Swiss roll tin, sprinkle with a pinch of flour, then spoon in the sponge mixture and bake in the preheated oven for 5 minutes. When baked, invert the sponge on to a scrupulously clean tea-towel and leave to cool.

Now prepare the custard. Heat the milk without letting it boil, and flavour with the lemon rind and remaining vanilla. In a bowl, whisk 4 egg yolks with 5 oz/150 g of the sugar and 2 oz/50 g of the flour. Gradually pour in the milk, stirring to prevent lumps from forming, then return the mixture to the milk pan and place over very moderate heat. Simmer the custard for 4-5 minutes, then take off the heat and leave to cool.

Meanwhile, put 3 egg whites in a bowl with the 6 oz/175 g sugar, then stand the bowl in a saucepan filled with 2 fingers of tepid water. Place over very moderate heat and whisk the egg whites in the bain-marie until very firm. Whip 14 fl oz/400 ml of the cream separately until very stiff. Delicately fold the whipped cream, Maraschino and finally the beaten egg whites into the cold custard.

Line the base of a 9 inch/23 cm springform cake tin with a circle of greaseproof paper. Cover the sides with a strip of sponge cake. Pour all the custard into the prepared mould, then cover it with the remaining trimmings from the sponge. Cover with thick foil, then place in the freezer for at least 4 hours.

Just before serving, make a raspberry sauce. Purée the raspberries with the remaining 3 oz/75 g sugar and a tablesoon of Maraschino liqueur, then transfer to a bowl. Remove the base and foil from the mould and unmould the semifreddo on to a serving plate. Remove the paper circle and decorate the dessert with swirls of whipped cream and sugar shapes. Serve the semifreddo immmediately, accom-panied by the raspberry sauce.

Orange Tart with Whipped Cream (opposite) and *Semifreddo Ice Cream with Raspberry Sauce (right)*

Home-made Sultana Cake

Dolce Casereccio all'Uvetta

To make 2 cakes

about 5 oz/150 g butter, plus extra for greasing the mould and tin

12 oz/350 g flour, plus extra for the mould and tin and mixing with the sultanas

4 oz/100 g sultanas

3 tablespoons Strega liqueur

3 eggs, separated

5 oz/150 g caster sugar

salt

grated rind of 1 lemon

1 oz/25 g pine nuts

1 teaspoon baking powder

¹/₄ teaspoon vanilla essence

a little icing sugar

Preparation and cooking time: about 1¹/₄ hours

The above ingredients will make 2 cakes, each to serve 5-6 people. Preheat the oven to 350°F/180°C/gas mark 4. Butter and flour a round fluted 1¹/₄ pint/750 ml mould and a rectangular 9 x 5 inch/23 x 12 cm cake tin. Soak the sultanas in the Strega liqueur. Whip the egg yolks, setting the whites aside, with the caster sugar, a pinch of salt and the lemon rind.

When you have a light frothy mixture, incorporate 4 oz/100 g cooled melted butter, mixing constantly and vigorously. Continue beating for a few minutes, then drain the sultanas and add these, floured and mixed with the pine nuts. Sift in 8 oz/225 g of the flour mixed with the baking powder. Add the vanilla and 2 tablespoons of the Strega in which the sultanas were soaked.

Whisk the egg whites with a pinch of salt until they are firm and carefully fold into the mixture which should be fairly stiff. Pour half into each mould, shaking them lightly to eliminate air bubbles. Bake the rectangular cake for 30 minutes and the round one for

40 minutes. Remove from the oven and leave to cool.

Before serving, sprinkle one or both cakes with icing sugar. Serve with cream, or with zabaglione or custard. The cakes can be kept for 3-4 days in their moulds covered with foil. Leave in a cool place (not the refrigerator).

St. Valentine's Heart

Cuore di San Valentino

To serve 6-8

8 oz/225 g puff pastry

8 macaroons

4 oz/100 g chestnuts, boiled and puréed

2 oz/50 g icing sugar

2 tablespoons Amaretto liqueur

3 tablespoons very fresh Mascarpone cheese or cream cheese

$^1\!/_2$ oz/15 g cocoa powder

2 oz/50 g pine nuts

2 oz/50 g sultanas

2 eggs

$^1\!/_3$ pint/200 ml whipping cream

10 pink sugar almonds

1 tablespoon coloured sugar crystals

a little flour

Preparation and cooking time: $1^1\!/_2$ hours, plus any defrosting

Defrost the puff pastry if necessary, then roll it out to about $^1\!/_8$ inch/3 mm thick. Roll it round the rolling pin, then unroll it on to a baking tray. Place a mould or a piece of cardboard cut into a heart shape that almost covers the pastry on top, and cut around it with a sharp knife. Discard the pastry trimmings. Prick the heart with a fork and leave to rest.

Meanwhile, preheat the oven to 375°F/190°C/ gas mark 5. Crumble 6 of the macaroons finely and put in a bowl with the puréed chestnuts, 1 oz/25 g sifted sugar, the Amaretto liqueur, the Mascarpone cheese and the cocoa powder. Stir well until smooth and creamy, then mix in the pine nuts and 1 oz/25 g washed and dried sultanas. Bind the mixture with the eggs, beating vigorously.

Spread over the puff pastry to about $^1\!/_2$ inch/1 cm from the edge. Bake on a low shelf for about 20 minutes.

Place the heart on a rack to cool. Meanwhile, crumble the rest of the macaroons very finely. Whip the cream until it is quite stiff, then put it into a piping bag fitted with a round, fluted nozzle. Pipe rosettes round the edge of the heart. Sieve the remaining icing sugar over the top, then decorate the cake with the rest of the sultanas, the remaining crumbled macaroons, the pink sugar almonds and the coloured sugar crystals. Serve immediately.

St.Valentine's Heart (above)

Love Hearts

Biscottini d'Amore

To serve 6

8 oz/225 g flour, plus a little extra for rolling

a pinch of salt

a pinch of ground cinnamon

a pinch of ground cloves

grated rind of $^1\!/_2$ lemon

3 oz/75 g sugar

1 teaspoon baking powder

1 egg

1 teaspoon vanilla essence

4 oz/100 g butter, softened and diced, plus a little extra

1 heaped teaspoon cocoa powder

1 teaspoon brandy

icing sugar for decorating (optional)

Preparation and cooking time: about 1 hour

Mix the flour with the salt, cinnamon and cloves, lemon rind and sugar. Add the baking powder. Then make a well in the centre and add the whole egg, the vanilla essence and the butter.

Knead all together quickly to give a smooth, even dough, then divide into 2 pieces, one twice as large as the other. Work 1 heaped teaspoon of sieved cocoa powder into the smaller piece of dough together with the brandy, kneading for a few minutes. Roll the larger piece out on the board sprinkled lightly with flour to a thickness of about $^1\!/_8$ inch/3 mm. Then cut into shapes using a heart-shaped pastry cutter and arrange them on 1 or 2 buttered and floured baking trays. Knead together the remaining dough, roll out and cut out more shapes. Continue until all the dough has been used. Preheat the oven to 350°F/ 180°C/gas mark 4.

Now roll out the cocoa-flavoured dough and cut smaller heart shapes out of that, placing them centrally on top of the first hearts and pressing them down lightly to keep in place.

Lastly place the biscuits in the oven for about 12 minutes or until they are baked and a light golden brown. Remove carefully from the tray using a palette knife and allow to cool on a rack. If desired, sprinkle with a little icing sugar before serving.

Meringue Gâteau

Torta Meringata

To serve 10

a little oil for greasing paper

4 eggs, plus 3 extra whites

salt

8 oz/225 g icing sugar, plus extra for sprinking

vanilla sugar

4 oz/100 g flour, plus extra for dusting the tray

1 oz/25 g butter, diced

4 oz/100 g sugar

1 pint/600 ml milk

1 tablespoon cocoa powder

1 tablespoon Grand Marnier

1 tablespoon Maraschino liqueur

4 fl oz/100 ml whipping cream

Preparation and cooking time:
about 4 hours

To prepare the meringue, lightly grease an 11 inch/28 cm circle of greaseproof paper with a little oil and place it on a small baking tray. Preheat the oven to 225°F/130°C/gas mark 1.

Whisk 3 egg whites with a pinch of salt and sieve in 7 oz/200 g of the icing sugar and a little vanilla sugar, a little at a time, beating briskly until the mixture is well risen and firm. Using a piping bag with a round nozzle, cover the circle of greaseproof paper by piping two overlapping spirals. Sprinkle the remaining icing sugar on top, then bake for a couple of hours; then turn off the oven and leave for an hour before taking it out to cool.

To prepare the éclairs, preheat the oven to 375°F/190°C/gas mark 5, and butter and flour a small baking tray. Bring 5 tablespoons of water to the boil in a saucepan with the diced butter and a pinch of salt. As soon as the butter is melted, remove from the heat and sieve in 2 oz/50 g of the flour, beating briskly with a wooden spoon. Return the pan to the heat and continue to cook, stirring continuously, until the mixture begins

to sizzle and comes away from the side of the pan. Turn it on to a plate and spread it out to cool.

Return the cooled mixture to the pan and beat in 1 egg, making sure the mixture is completely smooth. Using a piping bag with a round nozzle, pipe at least 30 finger shapes on the prepared baking tray, spaced apart to allow them to spread. Bake for 15 minutes, then turn them out to cool on a wire rack.

To prepare the custard, beat the remaining eggs, the sugar, a little vanilla sugar, the remaining flour and a pinch of salt together in a saucepan. When smooth, gradually stir in the milk. Bring to the boil, stirring all the time. Remove from the heat and divide into 2 portions, adding the cocoa powder and Grand Marnier to one half and the Maraschino liqueur to the other. Let them cool, stirring frequently, then put them into 2 piping bags with round nozzles.

To assemble the gâteau, whip the cream and pipe it into the éclairs, then sprinkle them with a little icing sugar. Just before serving, set the meringue base on a large plate, make a ring round the edge with the yellow custard and set the éclairs on it. Cover the rest of the meringue with alternate stripes of both custards and serve.

Meringue Gâteau

Pistachio and Coffee Cake

Cake con Pistacchio e Caffè

coffee liqueur

4 teaspoons instant coffee granules

9 oz/250 g butter, softened

9 oz/250 g icing sugar

4 eggs, separated

10 oz/300 g flour

a pinch of salt

4 oz/100 g pistachios, shelled and finely chopped

flour and butter for the tin

Preparation and cooking time: about 1¹/₂ hours

Preheat the oven to 350°F/180°C/gas mark 4. Heat the liqueur and dissolve the coffee powder in it. Leave to cool. With an electric mixer, beat the butter with the sugar to a smooth cream.

Then add the egg yolks, one at a time. Sift in 9 oz/250 g of the flour from a height. Beat the egg whites with the salt until very stiff.

Divide the cake mixture into 2 equal portions; fold half the egg whites and the chopped pistachios into one portion and the cold coffee liqueur and the remaining egg whites into the other. Generously grease and flour a rectangular 5 x 12 inch/12 x 30 cm cake tin and divide it along its length with a piece of cardboard. Put half the pistachio mixture in one section and half the coffee mixture in the other, then reverse the 2 colours. Remove the cardboard divider and bake for 1 hour 10 minutes.

Fig and Apricot Ring

Torta 'Coroncina'

To serve 8-10

extra butter and flour for the tin

3 eggs

5 oz/150 g caster sugar

2 sachets vanilla sugar

a pinch of salt

4 oz/100 g flour

2 oz/50 g potato flour

3 large, very ripe figs

¹/₃ pint/200 ml whipping cream

¹/₄ pint/150 ml Cointreau

icing sugar

4 oz/100 g apricot jam

3 sprigs redcurrants

Preparation and cooking time: about 1¹/₄ hours

Preheat the oven to 350°F/180°C/gas mark 4. Butter and flour a round 12 inch/30 cm cake tin, such as a Kugelhopf pan. Whisk the eggs with the sugar, the vanilla sugar and salt until light and fluffy. Mix the flour and the potato flour and sift into the

Pistachio and Coffee Cake (below) and *Rich Zucotto* (opposite)

mixture. Fold in carefully using a wooden spoon with an up and down motion. Pour into the cake tin and bake for about 30 minutes until a wooden skewer pushed into the cake comes out clean. Turn out on to a rack and leave to cool.

Wipe the figs with a damp cloth, cut them in half and then into very thin slices using a small very sharp knife. Whip the cream until it is stiff.

Cut the cake into 4 equal layers. Place the bottom round on a serving dish and pour over one third of the Cointreau. Then spread over a third of the whipped cream. Sprinkle with a teaspoon of icing sugar. Repeat the procedure with the other two layers and lightly press on the fourth.

Decorate the top with the fig slices to form a coronet. Melt the apricot jelly over a low heat and when it is runny, sieve through a fine strainer and brush the figs with it. Leave until the jelly has cooled. Complete the decoration with the redcurrants and serve at once.

Rich Zucotto

Zuccotto Ricco

To serve 12

7 egg yolks

10 oz/300 g caster sugar

salt

¹/₂ teaspoon vanilla essence

7 oz/200 g flour

extra flour and butter for the tin

18 fl oz/500 ml milk

grated rind of ¹/₂ lemon

7 oz/200 g plain chocolate

14 fl oz/400 ml double cream

4 fl oz/100 ml Crème de Cacao liqueur

langue de chat **biscuits, for serving**

Preparation and cooking time:
about 2 hours, plus 3 hours' chilling

Preheat the oven to 375°F/190°C/gas mark 5. First make a sponge cake. (You can do this the day before.) Beat 3 egg yolks with 5 oz/150 g of the sugar and a pinch of salt until the mixture forms a ribbon. (When you lift the whisk, the mixture that falls from it does not sink back immediately into the mixture in the bowl, but remains lightly on the surface.) Stir in the vanilla, then sift on 5 oz/150 g of the flour from a height, folding in carefully. Pour the mixture into a buttered and floured 9 inch/23 cm cake tin, and bake in the oven for about 35 minutes,

or until a skewer inserted into the centre comes out clean. Remove from the oven, invert on to a wire rack and leave to cool.

Meanwhile, make the pastry cream. Beat 4 egg yolks with the remaining sugar and flour. Heat the milk with the lemon rind, then pour it into the egg mixture in a thin stream. Set over moderate heat and, stirring continuously, boil for about 5 minutes, then turn off the heat and leave to cool.

Melt 5 oz/150 g of the chocolate and cool until it is tepid. Whip one-quarter of the double cream until very firm and mix it with the chocolate and the cooled pastry cream.

To assemble the zuccotto, cut the crusts off the sponge cake and slice it. Moisten with the liqueur diluted with 4 fl oz/100 ml water. Use some of the slices to line a large, flat-bottomed bowl. Cut the rest into strips and fill the bowl with layers of chocolate cream and sponge strips. Chill in the refrigerator for at least 3 hours.

Unmould the zuccotto on to a serving plate. Whip the remaining cream, place in a piping bag with a ridged nozzle, and pipe it over the zuccotto. Melt the rest of the chocolate, place in an icing bag and decorate the zuccotto, finishing with a crown of *langues de chat* biscuits. Leave in the fridge until ready to serve; the decorated zuccotto will keep for about 6-8 hours.

Preparation and cooking time: about 1¼ hours, plus at least 2 hours' chilling

Preheat the oven to 350°F/180°C /gas mark 4. Butter and flour a springform cake tin about 10 inches/25 cm in diameter. Beat 3 eggs with 5 oz/150 g of the sugar, half the vanilla sugar and the salt until frothy. Add the flour and the potato flour sieved together through a fine sieve. Fold them in very gently with an up-and-down movement rather than a circular one using a wooden spoon. Pour the batter into the cake tin and bake in the oven for about 35 minutes, or until a skewer inserted into the centre comes out clean. Turn the cake out on to a rack to cool.

Meanwhile, soften the gelatine in a little cold water. In a copper bowl, beat the 4 egg yolks together with the remaining sugar and vanilla sugar. When the mixture is frothy add the Marsala, making sure that each tablespoon is thoroughly absorbed before adding the next. Then add 3 tablespoons of the Amaretto liqueur, pouring it in a trickle and stirring all the time. Place the copper bowl over a pan of barely simmering water and, still stirring, heat the zabaglione cream until it is very hot. At this point remove it from the heat and fold in the gelatine. Mix thoroughly until the gelatine dissolves, then pour the zabaglione cream into a bowl and let it cool.

Cut the cake into 3 layers of equal thickness and place the lowest one back in the tin used to bake it, lined with greaseproof paper. Sprinkle the cake with a third of the remaining Amaretto liqueur and spread over it a third of the warm zabaglione cream. Repeat the same procedure with the second and third layers of cake. Refrigerate the cake for a least 2 hours, when the zabaglione cream will have set.

Beat the cream until stiff and put it in a piping bag. Wipe the strawberries and hull 4 of them, then cut them in half lengthways. Slide the blade of a small knife between the side of the mould and the cake, then open the hinge and detach the side of the mould. Slide the cake on to a serving dish by removing first the bottom of the mould and then the greaseproof paper. Decorate the top with the whipped cream and the strawberries. Serve immediately.

Mother's Day Cake

Torta 'Festa della Mamma'

To serve 10-12	**a pinch of salt**
butter and extra flour for the tin	**4 oz/100 g plain flour**
2 oz/50 g potato flour	**1 tablespoon powdered gelatine**
3 eggs, plus 4 extra yolks	**¼ pint/150 ml Marsala wine**
10 oz/300 g caster sugar	**¼ pint/150 ml Amaretto liqueur**
2 sachets of vanilla sugar	**¼ pint/150 ml whipping cream**
	5 large ripe strawberries

Festive Dove

Colomba Augurale

To serve 8

a little butter and flour for the tin

3 eggs, plus 6 egg yolks

12 oz/350 g caster sugar

¼ teaspoon honey

1 sachet vanilla sugar

a pinch of salt

4 oz/100 g flour

2 oz/50 g potato flour

1 pint/600 ml milk

1 tea bag

Preparation and cooking time: about 1½ hours

Preheat the oven to 350°F/180°C/gas mark 4. Butter and flour a dove-shaped cake tin, about 3 pints/1.8 litres in capacity. Whisk the 3 whole eggs with 5 oz/150 g of the sugar, the honey, the vanilla sugar and salt, until smooth and frothy. Mix the flour and potato flour and sift them into the sugar and egg mixture. Fold in with a wooden spoon using an up-and-down movement rather than a circular one so as not to deflate the mixture. Pour evenly into the tin and bake for about 30 minutes, until a skewer comes out clean. Remove the tin from the oven and, after a few minutes, turn the dove out on to a cooling rack.

While the cake is cooling, make the custard. Set aside 4 tablespoons of the milk and pour the rest into a saucepan. Bring gradually to the boil and remove from the heat. Put in the tea bag and leave to infuse for 5 minutes. Remove the tea bag, squeezing it thoroughly, and discard.

Beat the egg yolks with the remaining sugar until you obtain a frothy mixture. Then stir in first the reserved cold milk and then the tea-flavoured milk, poured in gradually through a fine strainer. Mix in with a small whisk. Heat the saucepan gently and bring the custard to just below boiling point, taking care not to let it actually boil. Remove from the heat at once and immerse in cold water, stirring continuously until the

custard has cooled.

Pour the custard into a jug or bowl and serve with the dove. Decorate the dove as you please.

Chocolate and Nut Gâteau

Veneziana con Panna e Castasgne

To serve 10

2¼ lb/1 kg large round brioche, panettone or plain cake

12 oz/350 g chestnuts, peeled and boiled

4 oz/100 g plain chocolate

2 oz/50 g walnuts

½ pint/300 ml whipping cream

4 oz/100 g icing sugar

¼ pint/150 ml rum

1 marron glacé

Preparation time: about 1 hour

Cut the cake into three equal layers. Purée the chestnuts (or use a can of already puréed unsweetened chestnuts.) Finely chop the chocolate and the walnuts. Whip the cream until stiff, then sift in 3 oz/75 g of the icing sugar, stirring with a top-to-bottom folding movement to avoid deflating the cream.

Place a layer of the cake on a serving plate, moisten it with half the rum, then spread it with half the whipped cream and half the chestnut purée, topped with half the chocolate and walnuts. Cover with the second layer of cake and fill in the same way. Cover with the top layer, place a small bowl in the centre and sprinkle the remaining icing sugar over the exposed surface of the cake. Remove the bowl and carefully place the marron glacé in the centre of the cake.

Serve as soon as possible without refrigerating. If you prefer, the cake may be cut into more layers — in which case the filling ingredients should be divided equally among all the layers.

Mother's Day Cake (opposite) and
Festive Dove (below)

Panettone Charlotte

Charlotte di Panettone

To serve 8

about 1 lb/450 g apples

about 1¹/₂ lb/675 g pears

4 oz/100 g butter, plus extra for the pudding basin

4 oz/100 g sugar

¹/₄ pint/150 ml dry white wine

12 oz/350 g panettone which has become a little hard

2 eggs

¹/₄ pint/150 ml milk

4 fl oz/100 ml double cream

Preparation and cooking time: about 2¹/₂ hours, plus cooling and chilling

Preheat the oven to 350°F/180°C/gas mark 4. Peel, core and quarter the apples and pears. Heat 2 frying pans with about 2 oz/50 g of the butter in each. As soon as the butter has melted, put the apples in one frying pan and the pears in the other. Sprinkle each with 1 tablespoon of sugar and pour half the wine into each frying pan. Cook over low heat until the fruit is cooked but still firm and the pieces intact.

Meanwhile, liberally butter a 3 pint/1.8 litre pudding basin, then cut two foil strips, about 2 inches/5 cm wide and long enough to place crossways inside the basin with about ³/₄ inch/2 cm at the ends to hang over the rim. Butter these, too.

Cut the panettone into thin slices. Place a layer of panettone on the bottom of the basin and press it down lightly to make it stick. Then place half the apples on top. Cover with another layer of panettone and then a layer of pears. Continue alternating the panettone, apples and pears in this way, finishing with a layer of panettone. Press down lightly so there are no spaces left.

Beat the eggs with the remaining sugar in a bowl and dilute with the milk and cream. Pour the mixture over the panettone and prick with a skewer to help the liquid penetrate. Leave the charlotte to rest for about 15 minutes,

then bake it for about 1¹/₂ hours. Remove from the oven and leave to cool.

Turn it out on to a serving dish with the help of the strips of foil (which should then be discarded). Refrigerate the charlotte for a couple of hours before serving. This is a particularly good recipe for using up leftover panettone.

Panettone Filled with Mandarin Orange Custard

Panettone Farcito al Mandarino

To serve 10-12

about 2 tablespoons powdered gelatine

4 eggs, separated

4 oz/100 g sugar

grated rind of 1 mandarin orange

2 oz/50 g flour

¹/₂ pint/300 ml milk

4 fl oz/100 ml mandarin juice

1 panettone

4 tablespoons Cointreau liqueur

14 fl oz/400 ml whipping cream

Preparation and cooking time: about 1 hour, plus 6-8 hours' chilling

Dissolve the gelatine in cold water. Whisk together the egg yolks and the sugar in a saucepan until pale and frothy. Add the mandarin orange rind, then sift in the flour. Mix again, then dilute with the milk and mandarin juice, adding them in a trickle. Bring slowly to the boil, stirring constantly with a wooden spoon. Remove from the heat and dissolve the gelatine in the mixture. Leave to cool, stirring gently from time to time to prevent a skin forming.

Meanwhile, turn the panettone upside-down and, using a sharp-pointed knife, cut out a circle from the base, about ³/₄ inch/2 cm from the edge. Make a large cavity and pour in the Cointreau. Whip the cream and fold it into the cold mandarin-flavoured custard. Use an up-and-

down movement, not a circular one, to prevent the cream from going flat. Pour the mixture into the panettone and replace the circle in the base to restore its original form. Place it upside-down in a bowl that is just the right size to hold the panettone and cover with cling film.

Refrigerate for 6-8 hours or, better still, overnight. Turn out on to a serving dish and serve. Cut with a sharp, serrated knife to avoid crumbling it.

Panettone with Sauce

Salsa di Panettone

To serve 12

10 oz/300 g mixed berries, such as strawberries, raspberries, blueberries

10 oz/300 g caster sugar

2 fl oz/50 ml Grand Marnier or other orange liqueur

1 x 2¹/₄ lb/1 kg panettone

Preparation: about 10 minutes, plus overnight marinating

Pick over the fruits and discard any that are bruised, then wash them thoroughly and drain well. Marinate overnight in the sugar and liqueur.

Just before serving, crush the fruits with a small whisk, leaving them in the marinade, and mix to obtain a thick sauce. Transfer to a bowl and bring to the table for your guests to help themselves. Slice the panettone into plain pieces (as it comes in the box), or cut into ³/₄ inch/2 cm slices and briefly toast in a very hot oven. Serve accompanied by the fruit sauce.

Panettone Filled with Mandarin Orange Custard (top) and Panettone Charlotte (bottom)

Home-made Apple Sponge

Torta di Mele, Casereccia

To serve 8

2 eggs

5 oz/150 g caster sugar

salt

grated rind of 1 lemon

a pinch of ground cinnamon

a pinch of ground cloves

5 oz/150 g flour

1 oz/25 g cornflour

5 tablespoons milk

1 teaspoon baking powder

butter for greasing the tin, plus a little extra

breadcrumbs

1 lb/500 g apples, just ripe

3 oz/75 g apricot jam

Preparation and cooking time: about 1½ hours, plus cooling

Preheat the oven to 350°F/180°C/gas mark 4. Beat the eggs with 4 oz/100 g of the sugar, a pinch of salt and the lemon rind. Then add another pinch of salt, followed by the cinnamon and the cloves. Combine the flour and the cornflour and sift these into the mixture. Gradually pour in the milk and sift in the baking powder. Mix all these ingredients together to form a smooth mixture.

Butter a 10 inch/25 cm cake tin and sprinkle it with breadcrumbs. Pour in the mixture. Peel and halve the apples, core and slice them, not too thinly. Arrange the slices on top of the mixture. Sprinkle with the remaining sugar and intersperse with slivers of butter. Bake for about 45 minutes or until a toothpick comes out clean. Remove the cake from the oven and leave to cool.

Heat the apricot jam over a low heat and, when it has melted, brush the surface of the cake with it and leave to cool. This cake is best eaten the same day.

Cherry Roulade

Roulade di Ciliegie

To serve 6

2 eggs, size 2

3 oz/75 g caster sugar

½ teaspoon vanilla essence

3 oz/75 g flour

butter for greasing the tin and greaseproof paper

½ pint/300 g whipping cream

icing sugar

orange flower water

9 oz/250 g cherries

Preparation and cooking time: about 40 minutes, plus chilling

To make the roulade sponge, preheat the oven to 400°F/200°C/gas mark 6. Whisk the eggs with the sugar and vanilla until light and fluffy, then sift in the flour from a height and fold it in.

Grease a 16 x 13½ inch/40 x 34 cm Swiss roll tin, line it with a sheet of greaseproof paper and lightly grease the paper. Pour in the sponge mixture and bake in the preheated oven for about 10 minutes.

Remove from the oven and invert the sponge on to a scrupulously clean tea-towel. Peel off the paper, roll up the sponge in the cloth and leave to cool.

Meanwhile, whip the cream very stiffly and flavour with 1 tablespoon of icing sugar and 1 tablespoon of orange flower water.

Rinse the cherries under running water, drain well and stone them, using a cherry stoner. Cut them into small pieces.

Unroll the sponge and spread over the cream. Sprinkle with the chopped cherries, then roll up again. Wrap the roulade in a sheet of greaseproof paper and refrigerate for at least 4 hours before serving. Cut the roulade into even slices and arrange these on a serving plate, decorating as you wish.

INDEX